ANCIENT
Greece

POCKET
MUSEUM

ANCIENT
Greece

DAVID MICHAEL SMITH

Thames & Hudson

Contents

Introduction

On the morning of 31 July 1801, a small six-man crew ascended wooden scaffolds to begin removal of a sculptural metope from the south side of the Temple of Athena Parthenos (the Parthenon) on the Athenian Acropolis. This metope, a panel of marble quarried from the Pentelikon range northeast of Athens, formed part of a Doric frieze depicting the mythological battle between the human Lapiths and the hybrid Centaurs. The six men, assisted by twenty Greeks, were employed by Thomas Bruce, Seventh Earl of Elgin and British Ambassador to the Ottoman Empire, who had been granted a letter of permit by the Ottoman Kaimakam at Constantinople allowing the drawing, casting and removal of architectural elements from the Acropolis. The task was evidently difficult, since a full day's effort secured only the single metope. By January 1804, however, Elgin had removed and exported sculptural elements from the Temples to Athena Parthenos and Athena Nike, the Erechtheion and the Propylaia, the monumental gateway to the sanctuary.

So began the most emotive and politicized episode of modern European cultural heritage. Interest in Greek antiquity, however, has a far longer history, having garnered attention from scholars, antiquarians and collectors for more than 2,000 years. Throughout, the Greek 'past' has existed in a state of near-constant reinvention and adaptation, revered or reviled in line with shifting political ideologies. Today, it is the foundation upon which Modern Greek cultural identity rests.

The Roman elite were avid consumers of Greek culture, and antiquities were removed to the private collections of prominent officials from the late Republic onwards. Ownership, much as in more recent history, reflected power, wealth and intellect. Pausanias records that Nero (54–68 CE) removed around 500 bronzes from the Sanctuary of Apollo at Delphi to Rome during his reign, and Novius Vindex is said to have possessed works by some of the most renowned sculptors of the Classical period. An entire sculptural industry emerged at Rome, providing marble copies of earlier Greek works to cater to demand. With the end of the Empire in the West, however, interest declined, facilitated by political unrest and a fledgling Christian orthodoxy that frowned upon 'pagan' culture and idolatry. Across Greece, history was subsumed into local folklore and monuments were left to decay and ruin; a handful, including the Parthenon, were appropriated by the Church.

The rediscovery of the Greek past began during the Renaissance, with the excavation at Rome – and beyond of some of the statuary that had so ignited the Imperial imagination, including the Apollo Belvedere and the Laocoön – and, by the later 16th century, an emergent taste for the geography, history and antiquities of Greece was apparent among the erudite of mainland Europe and, soon thereafter, Britain.

In 1675 French physician Jacques Spon and English botanist George Wheler undertook the first 'archaeological tour' of Greece proper, visiting Corinth, Eleusis, Marathon and Megara. They were among the first and last European antiquaries to see the Parthenon (a mosque since *c.* 1460) intact prior to its ruination by a Venetian force under Doge Morosini. The Ashmolean Museum was established at Oxford in 1683, and by the early 18th century, Greece had begun to attract the attention of more intrepid 'Grand Tourists': young male aristocrats, largely British, destined for political or military office. Major studies of the antiquities of Greece and Italy appeared later in the century, while Johann Winckelmann's *History of Art in Antiquity* (1764) prompted a sea change in the appreciation of Greek art. On 15 January 1759, the British Museum opened its doors as the first national public museum in the world.

The increased profile of Greece into the early 19th century saw the first American Grand Tourist, Philadelphian lawyer Nicholas Biddle, and the removal by European antiquarians of major sculptural works from Eleusis and Bassae. Others from Aegina were installed in the purpose-built Munich Glyptothek, while the Venus de Milo was installed in the Louvre. The French naval ensign responsible for the Venus's recovery, Olivier Voutier, would subsequently resign his commission and take up arms for Greece during the War of Independence (1821–30); one of hundreds, European and American, whose love of the Greek past translated to direct involvement in shaping its future.

PALAEOLITHIC TO EARLY BRONZE AGE	MIDDLE AND LATE BRONZE AGE
200,000 BCE	2100/2050 BCE

c. 200,000 BCE
First hominin occupation of Greece

c. 120,000 BCE
Appearance of Homo neanderthalensis in Greece

c. 40,000 BCE
Appearance of Anatomically Modern Humans in Greece

c. 13,000 BCE
Earliest exploitation of Melian obsidian

c. 7030 BCE
Arrival of the Neolithic at Knossos, Crete

c. 4800 BCE
First metal objects appear in the Aegean

c. 2100 BCE
Emergence of the first Minoan 'palaces'

c. 1627 BCE
Super-colossal eruption of Thera

c. 1420 BCE
Emergence of the first Mycenaean palaces

c. 1200 BCE
Collapse of the Mycenaean palace system

1190 BCE

With the creation of the Modern Greek state, archaeology in the country witnessed its coming of age. The export of antiquities was banned and the first National Museum established on Aegina (1829), the nation's first capital. The Greek Archaeological Service was established in 1833 and, buoyed by the Archaeological Society of Athens, began to extend study beyond the Classical into the more distant past. Construction of the National Archaeological Museum at Athens began in 1866. Foreign schools of archaeology were established at Athens and the first major foreign excavations were mounted under permit, led by the French at Delos (1873) and the Germans at Olympia (1875). The work of Heinrich Schliemann at Troy and Mycenae (legally from 1870 and 1876, respectively) thrust Greek Prehistory into the limelight, preluding the early 20th-century excavations of Sir Arthur Evans at Knossos.

Today, excavation continues to be carried out by the Greek Archaeological Service and by foreign institutes working under permit, while the application of new technologies and methodologies to material from both old and new excavations is allowing researchers a far greater understanding of the Greek past than ever before. This book presents almost 200 objects, housed within museum collections around the world, which together span from earliest prehistory to the close of the Hellenistic period. Groupings across five chronological chapters explore individual themes of society and household, art and personal adornment, politics and warfare, and funeral and ritual – utilizing the most up-to-date research to chart the development and destruction of the various cultures of the Greek world over the past 200,000 years.

ADRIATIC
SEA

Veii
Rome

Canosa

Fasano

Pithekoussai
Pompeii

Taras

Paestum

TYRRHENIAN
SEA

IONIAN
SEA

Riace

Gela
Syracuse

MEDITERRANEAN
SEA

Pangyurishte

Sindos
Vergina
Thessaloniki
Nea Nikomedia
Olynthus

Troy

Myrina

GREECE

Prodromos
Dodona
Dimini
Sesklo

Pergamon

AEGEAN
SEA

Kokkinopilos

Artemision

Lefkandi

Delphi
Thebes
Tanagra

Athens

Corinth
Isthmia
Mycenae
Kolonna
Argos
Dendra
Tiryns
Franchti Cave

Chalandriani

Delos

Olympia

Saliagos

Ialysos

Sparta
Pylos
Vapheio
Mavri Spilia

Phylakopi

Akrotiri

Antikythera

Malia
Mochlos
Palaikastro and Petsophas
Knossos
Kamares
Zakros
Aghia Triadha
Vasiliki
Phaistos

From Foraging to Farming

Discovered in the northern Greek cave of Petralona in September 1960, this controversial skull probably belonged to a mature male Homo heidelbergensis *which died between 150,000 and 350,000 years ago. It is among the earliest, if not the earliest, hominin fossil known from Greece.*

During the Lower Palaeolithic, Greece was occupied by bands of hunter-gatherers, perhaps *Homo heidelbergensis* or *H. erectus*. Evidence of their presence consists overwhelmingly of stone tools made in the Acheulean tradition. Examples from Rodia and Kokkinopilos are at least 200,000 years old; tools from Lesbos and Corfu may be older still. A new Middle Palaeolithic 'Mousterian' tool-making tradition marks the presence of Neanderthals in Greece, while more advanced Uluzzian and Aurignacian traditions subsequently signal the arrival of anatomically modern humans. Briefly, the two species coexisted, although decreased genetic diversity and increased resource competition contributed to the extinction of *H. neanderthalensis* by *c.* 39,000 BCE.

During the last major cold phase of the Würm Glaciation, new ideas emerged surrounding self-image, the treatment of the dead and sense of place. As the glaciers retreated, rising sea levels advanced the coastline inland. Climate change impacted animal and plant species, and thus hunting and foraging behaviours. By the start of the Mesolithic, the predilection for coastal foraging and fishing paralleled an increase in maritime activity, visible in the circulation of Melian obsidian and Saronic andesite, and the foundation of a seasonal village at Maroulas on Kythnos.

The Neolithic period represents a technological and cultural watershed characterized by the presence of domesticated plant and animal species within the first permanent agricultural villages. At Knossos, Neolithic technology appeared *c.* 7030 BCE, probably transmitted from Anatolia, either by settlers or trading contacts who shared knowledge and materials. It was present at Franchthi on the mainland by *c.* 6740 BCE and arrived in northern Greece by *c.* 6500 BCE. It was adopted enthusiastically in the fertile region of Thessaly, where settlements of approximately 100 to 300 people were separated by as little as 3 km (1¾ mi).

Among the most significant corollaries of this new Neolithic way of life was the manufacture of pottery. Early Neolithic vessels are few in number and simple in shape and decoration. By the Middle Neolithic, however, some vessels are finely executed. The emphasis is on display as pottery adopted a new importance for reinforcing common group identities, and certain styles, along with other craft products, were traded over long distances. During the Late Neolithic, some settlements show a shift towards increased

Waterlogged conditions at the Middle Neolithic lakeside settlement of Dispilio have preserved a variety of extraordinary artefacts. This reconstruction of the village, including housing platforms that extended into the lake, offers some idea of its original appearance.

These Middle and Late Neolithic arrowheads from Kouphovouno were made from obsidian and honey flint. They reflect the fact that hunting continued to supplement a Neolithic diet based largely on agro-pastoralism.

social differentiation. Provisions for cooking and the long-term storage of agricultural goods by families suggest a new sense of ownership over what was produced and how it was used, as the household became increasingly important. Some individuals may have derived power from their control of agricultural surplus. The Late Neolithic witnesses the first permanent settlement of the Cyclades, alongside movement into upland and agriculturally marginal areas on Crete and the mainland. Metal objects began to circulate in the Aegean that attest to links between Anatolia, Greece and the Balkans. A preference for coastal settlement in southern Greece during the Final Neolithic may reflect a desire to access maritime networks perhaps at the expense of exchange relationships with sites in Thessaly where settlement declined sharply, although the stone fortifications at some sites suggests that involvement was not without risk.

During the Early Bronze Age, distinct cultural identities emerged on the Greek mainland, Crete and the Cycladic archipelago, paralleling an increase in social, cultural and political complexity in an environment of expanding exchange networks and technological innovation. Most of the smaller Cycladic islands were colonized and major settlements are visible on Syros, Kea, Naxos and Ios. A thriving Cycladic craft economy emerged, paralleled by trade across the Aegean. Though some individuals may have risen to prominence, the lack of evidence for 'chiefly' elites suggests that the maintenance of relationships between islands required a different form of organization.

Similar developments in trade, settlement and craft activity are seen on Crete, although there are regional differences. Several coastal sites show close ties with the Cyclades. New types of built tomb appear and imported goods accompanied the dead as the act of burial became increasingly important in marking differences in wealth and social status. Reorganization and construction at Knossos, Malia and Phaistos anticipated the emergence of the later 'palatial' centres. Serious disruption marked the end of the Early Bronze Age on the mainland and in the Cyclades, while Crete largely witnessed a cultural quickening that heralded the emergence of the Minoan 'palace' proper.

Bifacial handaxe

at least *c.* 200,000 BCE
*Flint • Length: 15 cm (6 in.) • Late Lower
Palaeolithic • From Kokkinopilos, Epirus, Greece*
ARCHAEOLOGICAL MUSEUM
OF ARTA, GREECE

Evidence from Georgia, Bulgaria and Spain
demonstrates the migration of archaic
hominins across Europe more than a million
years ago. Tool-yielding sediment beds
at Kokkinopilos attest their presence in
Greece by at least *c.* 200,000 BCE, and even
earlier dates have been proposed for other
sites. Acheulean handaxes such as this were
probably used by several species of archaic
human; hunter-gatherers who followed
seasonal game trails across vast territories.
Kokkinopilos was an open-air camp located
at the edge of a seasonal lake, perhaps visited
only as meltwater attracted game species from
surrounding plains. Chopping tools such as
this would have been used to butcher prey.

Mousterian leaf point

c. 120,000–30,000 BCE
Flint • Length: 5 cm (2 in.) • Middle
Palaeolithic • From the Cave of Mavri Spilia,
Mani, Laconia, Greece

EPHORATE OF PALAEOANTHROPOLOGY
AND SPELEOLOGY OF SOUTHERN
GREECE, ATHENS, GREECE

The Middle Palaeolithic period in
Greece, as with the rest of Europe,
is recognized by the appearance
of another mode of stone-tool
production. 'Mousterian' tools
represent a further leap in technical
ability and contained a number of
new tool types, including large,
elongated points, such as this,
which were probably hafted and
used as spears. More significantly,
the Mousterian tool making
tradition is associated with
Homo neanderthalensis or
'Neanderthal man', fossil
remains of which are currently
confined to the Mani Peninsula.

Bowl

c. 6500–5800 BCE
*Ceramic • Height: 6.2 cm (2½ in.),
diameter at rim: 14.4 cm (5¾ in.) • Early
Neolithic • From Karatzadagli, Thessaly, Greece*

NATIONAL ARCHAEOLOGICAL MUSEUM,
ATHENS, GREECE

Although there is evidence for earlier experimentation with fired
clay, pottery production proper began in the Early Neolithic period.
Pots were handmade and fired in open bonfires, rather than kilns.
Early clay recipes show considerable variation as people sought
to understand the potential of this new technology. At this stage
production was probably relatively infrequent. Bowls with simple
monochrome decoration represent the most common vessel type.
This example may have been shaped in a wooden mould.

Biconical spindle whorl

c. 5800–5300 BCE
*Terracotta • Height: 2.5 cm (1 in.), diameter: 3.8 cm
(1½ in.) • Middle Neolithic • From Sesklo, Thessaly, Greece*

ARCHAEOLOGICAL MUSEUM OF VOLOS, GREECE

There is no evidence for the systematic and intensive
exploitation of secondary animal products (milk,
wool) during the earlier Neolithic, although both
whorls for maintaining the speed of the spindle and
weights for keeping the warp thread taught on the
loom provide evidence for the domestic production
of textiles, probably using wool as well as flax. Like
other Neolithic crafts, weaving may have become
increasingly specialized, and it is very likely that
textiles were traded between communities.

Axe head

c. 6500–1050 BCE

Stone • Length: 3.6 cm (1½ in.)
• Neolithic–Bronze Age • Provenance
unknown (said to be from the area
of Thessaloniki, Greece)

BRITISH MUSEUM,
LONDON, UK

Ground stone tools formed a major component of the Neolithic toolkit. The use to which they were put would have been dictated, in part, by the properties of the stone from which they were manufactured. Some would have been used to clear woodland for the planting of new Neolithic crop species, others perhaps for preparing the soil. Others still could have been used for woodworking, the preparation of skins and various other tasks that accompanied the shift to agriculture and settled village life. The small size of many examples is probably the result of frequent re-sharpening. Some examples may have had symbolic value.

BEADS, PENDANTS AND AMULETS

c. 6740–5500 BCE

Shell and stone • Dimensions: various • Early–Middle Neolithic
• From Franchthi Cave, Southern Argolid, Greece

ARCHAEOLOGICAL MUSEUM OF NAFPLION, GREECE

As the earliest Neolithic site on the mainland, Franchthi Cave remains hugely important for our understanding of the adoption of Neolithic technology across Greece. It also provides arguably our earliest evidence for craft specialization, in an industry focused on the production of shell beads. Hundreds of shell blanks have been excavated, broken or discarded during the manufacturing process, alongside hundreds of lithic points and borers, which were used for roughing out and drilling. Production was perhaps undertaken by those members of the community who simply chose to profit from their spare time by exploiting an abundant local resource. The large number of tools compared with the small number of finished beads suggests that some of these objects were exported, perhaps through quite extensive exchange networks. Production of this sort was made possible by the shift towards permanent settlement that accompanied the arrival of Neolithic technology. This shift also saw developments in social behaviour and spiritual belief, which were catered to by an increasingly elaborate range of shell and stone beads, pendants and other ornaments.

Franchthi Cave in the Southern Argolid was occupied during the very late Mesolithic and the earliest stages of the Neolithic. The remains of plants and animals from the site provide an important opportunity to study the shift from hunting and foraging to sedentism and agriculture.

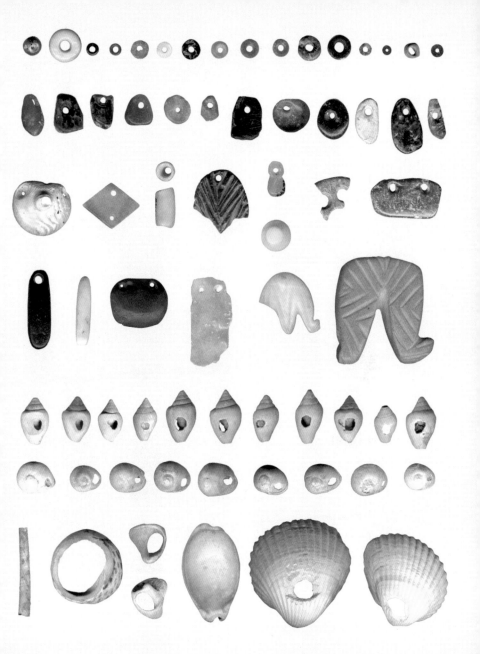

House model

c. 5500–5300 BCE

*Terracotta • Length: 9 cm (3½ in.),
width: 7 cm (2¾ in.) • Middle
Neolithic • From Krannon
(Douraki), Thessaly, Greece*

ARCHAEOLOGICAL
MUSEUM OF VOLOS, GREECE

The average Early Neolithic Thessalian village probably supported between 100 and 300 inhabitants. Many would have lived in single-storey, single-room structures of mud brick or pise (rammed earth), or wattle and daub on a timber frame. Floors were often of beaten earth, although some may have been planked or covered with reed matting. Shelves, benches and bins provided storage, while hearths were used for cooking and heating. More complex structures, with extra rooms and perhaps mezzanine levels or second storeys, appeared in the Middle Neolithic. This model may represent an idealized version of a typical house, or a building with some ritual or symbolic significance.

Solid Style cup

c. 5500–5300 BCE

Ceramic • Height: 14.8 cm (5¾ in.), diameter at rim: 17.3 cm (6¾ in.)
• Middle Neolithic • From Tzani Magoula, Karditsa, Thessaly, Greece

ARCHAEOLOGICAL MUSEUM OF VOLOS, GREECE

Pottery production increased dramatically during the Middle
Neolithic. Potters exhibited a greater technical understanding
of clays and tempers, and it is possible that some were operating
as specialists. Vessels related to the serving and consumption
of foodstuffs, including bowls, cups and jars, continued to form
the focus of production, and some styles enjoyed popularity
over substantial areas. Other needs could have been met by
vessels and containers made of wood, leather or basketry, and
it has been suggested that some of the incised and painted
geometric motifs that appeared during this phase may have
been designed in imitation.

Dimini Ware bowl

c. 4800–4500 BCE
Ceramic • Dimensions: unknown • Late Neolithic
• From Dimini, Thessaly, Greece
ARCHAEOLOGICAL MUSEUM OF VOLOS, GREECE

The later Neolithic period in Thessaly is characterized by
an extraordinary density of occupation, with substantial
settlements often located no more than a few kilometres
apart. In this highly networked landscape, the production
and consumption of pottery and other material culture played
an important role in negotiating both individual and group
identities and social relationships within and between sites.
Dimini Ware is characteristic of the Late Neolithic period in
eastern Thessaly, although it was traded and imitated outside
the region and has been identified as far away as Cakran in
Albania. This bowl and its abstract decoration are typical
of the highly standardized 'Classical' Dimini style.

Globular jar

c. 5300–4800 BCE

Ceramic • Height: 25 cm (9¾ in.), diameter at rim: 12 cm (4¾ in.) • Late Neolithic • From Dimini, Thessaly, Greece

NATIONAL ARCHAEOLOGICAL MUSEUM,
ATHENS, GREECE

It has been argued that Late Neolithic society saw a shift in emphasis from collective, communal identity to individual household identity. Previously open-air cooking facilities, which would have seen food prepared in view of, and presumably shared with, neighbours are moved within buildings or property boundaries, and there are hints elsewhere of a greater focus on the individual household. Technically and artistically accomplished, this jar may have served a special function in collective feasting activities designed to reinforce household identities or inter-household relationships.

Female figurine

c. 6500–5800 BCE

Terracotta • Height: 6.8 cm (2¾ in.), width: 9.1 cm (3½ in.)
• Early Neolithic • From Prodromos, Karditsa, Thessaly, Greece
ARCHAEOLOGICAL MUSEUM OF VOLOS, GREECE

The majority of Early Neolithic figurines constitute schematic
or more or less naturalistic female types that adopt static poses.
This example is unusual in that it depicts a figure in action:
a female carrying a basket across her shoulders. The basket
is pierced, which suggests that it may have formed the spout
of a jug. Simply modelled human faces in relief occasionally
decorate the walls of Early Neolithic vessels in northern
Greece, although the addition of a human figure is exceptional
for the period.

Blade core

c. 3100–2200 BCE
*Obsidian • Length: 10.2 cm (4 in.) • Early
Cycladic I–II • From Antiparos, Cyclades*
BRITISH MUSEUM, LONDON, UK

Throughout the Neolithic and earlier
Bronze Age, obsidian constituted the most
important raw material for the production
of lithic blades across southern and central
Greece. Outcrops of this volcanic glass at
Sta Nychia and Demenegaki on the Cycladic
island of Melos were exploited by the
inhabitants of Franchthi during the Upper
Palaeolithic (*c.* 13,000 BCE), and continued
to form the primary Aegean obsidian source
during later periods. Pre-prepared cores such
as this moved throughout the Aegean during
the Early Bronze Age, some perhaps carried
by craftsmen who moved from village to
village producing blades as required.

Hut pyxis

c. 3100–2200 BCE
Steatite • Length: 14.8 cm (5¾ in.), height: 7.2 cm (2¾ in.)
• Early Cycladic I–II • From Naxos, Cyclades
NATIONAL ARCHAEOLOGICAL MUSEUM, ATHENS, GREECE

This vessel belongs to a category of elaborately decorated pyxides that appear to mimic the design of Early Cycladic architecture, with examples variously identified as domestic structures, sacred buildings or granaries. It is possible that all types are represented. The long-term storage of grain would have been a vital strategy for a typical marginal Early Cycladic agricultural community, and the importance of the household and the divine are obvious, although the value of such symbolism on a vessel that perhaps held jewelry or cosmetics is not clear. Not all known examples have a secure provenance, although most were probably grave goods and may have served a sepulchral function.

Longboat model

c. 2750–2200 BCE

*Lead • Length: 35.9 cm (14¼ in.), width: 3.9 cm
(1½ in.) • Early Cycladic II • Provenance unknown*

WORLD MUSEUM, LIVERPOOL, UK

The longboat was arguably one of the core
elements of Early Cycladic society. It was
likely just one type among a larger range
of seacraft that populated the waters of the
archipelago, although their preferential
depiction in Early Cycladic art suggests they
may have enjoyed a uniquely high status.
Estimated at 15–20 m (49–65 ft) in length,
with a minimum complement of perhaps
twenty-five rowers, they were poorly suited
to carrying bulk cargos and may have been
reserved for more specialist activities, such
as raiding or ritual. The manpower required
to crew a boat of this type may have seen
its use restricted to a handful of larger
Cycladic communities.

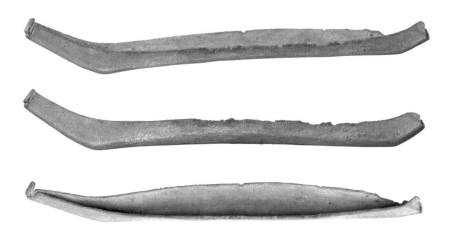

'FRYING PANS'

c. 2750–2200 BCE

Ceramic • Height: 6 cm (2¼ in.), diameter: 28 cm (11 in.) • Early Cycladic II
• From Chalandriani, Syros, Cyclades

NATIONAL ARCHAEOLOGICAL MUSEUM, ATHENS, GREECE

While named for their similarity to the modern frying pan, there is no evidence to suggest these vessels were used for cooking. Most examples have been recovered from cemeteries and a variety of other interpretations have been suggested, including their use as ritual containers for food offerings, plates, salt-moulds, mirrors and drums. The presence of decoration on the underside of these vessels suggests that, for full effect, they would have been raised, hung or mounted.

This example is one of the most impressive. The central motif is that of a longboat at sea; the fish totem raised high on the stern may represent a navigational aid. The depiction of female genitalia below the ship is a common pairing at Chalandriani, one of the few communities considered large enough to have meaningfully employed the longboat, and establishes a conceptual link between the sea and biological reproduction or fertility. This may be in reference to a female deity whose attributes linked her to the sea, or to more pragmatic concerns of social reproduction and exogamous marriage. The inclusion of female genitalia, combined with the leg-like forked handles of this example, lend the pan an anthropomorphic character.

A variety of impressed and incised motifs decorate the surface of Early Cycladic II frying pans. Alongside depictions of longboats, these can include birds, fish, stars or the sun, as well as multiple interlocking spirals representing the sea. All are closely connected to maritime activity.

Vasiliki Ware
teapot and cup

c. 2400–2200 BCE
Ceramic • Height of teapot: 17 cm (6¾ in.),
height of cup: 8.5 cm (3¼ in.) • Early Minoan IIB
• Vasiliki, Crete

BRITISH MUSEUM, LONDON, UK (TEAPOT);
HERAKLION ARCHAEOLOGICAL MUSEUM,
CRETE, GREECE (CUP)

Pottery manufacture during the Early Minoan period is characterized by its regionality. Several distinct styles appear on the island and have a limited presence beyond the regions in which they were produced. Vasiliki Ware, however, is relatively widespread. Its mottled surface reflects an early attempt to manipulate firing conditions within the kiln. It may have been intended to mirror the appearance of vessels in stone, which became popular in eastern Crete during the same period. The style is closely associated with new shapes that appear at the same time, including the so-called 'teapot' shown here.

Zoomorphic pyxis

c. 3100–2200 BCE
Marble • Height: 4 cm (1½ in.), length: 12.7 cm (5 in.)
• Early Cycladic I–II • Provenance unknown
(said to be from Naxos, Cyclades)

GOULANDRIS MUSEUM OF CYCLADIC ART,
ATHENS, GREECE

Zoomorphic stone vessels are extremely rare in the
Early Bronze Age Cyclades, and this porcine pyxis
is an exceptional example. It may have held pigment
or unguents, and would have been sealed with a lid.
The choice of animal is unusual. Pigs were ubiquitous
in the islands, although they were far outnumbered
by sheep and goats, which were better suited to the
difficult conditions and which provided secondary
products such as milk and fleece. Pigs yielded only
meat and represented a significant investment
in a marginal environment.

Silver bracelet

c. 3100–2100 BCE
Silver • Diameter: 5.3 cm (2 in.),
weight: 9.55 g • Early Cycladic II–III
• Provenance unknown
(said to be from Pholegandros)

Hammered into shape from a single strip of sheet silver, this undecorated strip-type open loop bracelet was, like much Early Cycladic silver, purportedly recovered from a grave. Although metal objects circulated in the Aegean from the later Neolithic, silver becomes far more visible during the Early Bronze Age, reflecting both an evolution in metallurgical technology and exploitation of the principal Cycladic silver source at Ayios Sostis on Siphnos. Small, personal items – pins, necklaces, toilet implements and, less commonly, bracelets – dominate the silversmith's repertoire; catering to an emergent market for high-status adornment and perhaps responding to influence from the eastern Aegean.

Spouted bowl

c. 2750–2200 BCE
Marble • Diameter: 12.7 cm (5 in.) • Early Cycladic II
• Provenance unknown
GOULANDRIS MUSEUM OF CYCLADIC ART,
ATHENS, GREECE

The use of pigment in the Aegean can be traced
back as far as the Upper Palaeolithic, when the iron
oxide ochre was intensively mined at Tzines on the
island of Thasos. A much wider range of mineral
pigments were employed during the Early Cycladic
period, traces of which are commonly preserved
on the vessels and tools used in their preparation.
This spouted bowl likely came from a grave,
and the thick residue of the copper
compound azurite may well
represent pigment applied
to the body prior to or
during burial.

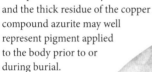

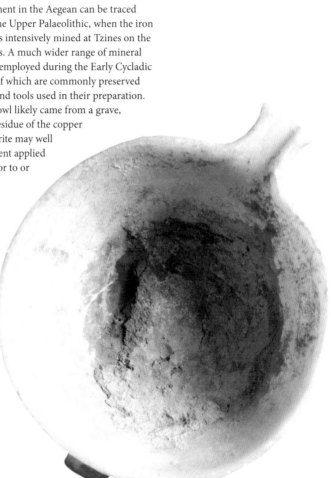

Bone tube

c. 2750–2200 BCE
*Bone • Length: 10.2 cm (4 in.),
diameter: 1.5 cm (½ in.) • Early
Cycladic II • Naxos, Cyclades
(exact provenance unknown)*

NATIONAL ARCHAEOLOGICAL
MUSEUM, ATHENS, GREECE

Modification of the body through tattooing, painting
or scarification was probably used in the Early
Cycladic period, as it is today, to indicate membership
of a particular social group, to mark a particular life
stage or to memorialize a particular event. Pigment
containers are occasionally found as grave offerings,
accompanied in rare instances by copper needles and
obsidian tools that could have been used to introduce
colour under the skin. Rare or toxic pigments may
have been restricted to special events or individuals.
This tube contains azurite, the popularity of which
was probably linked to the development of copper
metallurgy in the archipelago and the exploitation
of copper ore deposits. It may even have possessed
a symbolic value precisely because of the association.

Head of a folded-arm figurine

c. 2750–2200 BCE
Marble • Length: 22.8 cm (9 in.) • Early Cycladic II
• Provenance unknown

J. PAUL GETTY MUSEUM, MALIBU, USA

Scientific analyses using ultraviolet and infrared light have made clear that the marble figurines of the Early Cycladic period could be painted and repainted over the course of their use-life with multiple anatomical features, articles of jewelry, headgear, hair and abstract motifs perhaps representative of real-world body-modification. These objects may well have been used in public settings, where the choice of motifs, and even the choice of pigment, could have conveyed information about their owner. Specific motifs may have been suitable only for certain occasions, such as death and burial.

GOLD JEWELRY

c. 2750–2200 BCE

Gold • Dimensions: various • Early Minoan II (–III) • From Mochlos, Crete

HERAKLION ARCHAEOLOGICAL MUSEUM, CRETE, GREECE

The Early Minoan settlement on the island of Mochlos has been characterized as a gateway community. Though today an island, during the Early Bronze Age the settlement occupied a promontory, joined to the mainland and flanked by a pair of harbours that provided it with a privileged access to maritime trade networks. The site itself ranks among the largest of the period, and the rich contents of its cemetery betray the prosperity of some of its inhabitants. The cemetery was positioned on the seaward side of the hill, visible to approaching ships but not from the settlement. It included a series of so-called house tombs – structures that, in some respects resemble domestic buildings, but which were not clearly envisaged as a house for the dead. More monumental three-roomed tombs were located on a western terrace, distinguished in space and perhaps by the status of their occupants. These tombs were used for multiple burials over an extended period, with primary inhumations eventually collected and grouped together with the bones of earlier interments. Grave offerings included jewelry and other objects in gold – such as this daisy-head pin and olive-leaf spray – and silver, stone vessels and pottery, although the nature of these tombs presents difficulties for their dating and the identification of particular offerings with individual remains.

The site of Mochlos was one of several settlements on the North Cretan coast that prospered from maritime trade with the Cyclades during the Early Bronze Age and typifies many of the processes that would subsequently lead to the development of the major 'palatial' centres.

Slotted spearhead

c. 2750–2200 BCE

*Copper • Length: 19 cm (7½ in.) • Early
Cycladic II • From Stavros, Amorgos, Cyclades*

NATIONAL ARCHAEOLOGICAL MUSEUM,
ATHENS, GREECE

The Early Cycladic II period witnessed
both an increase in the proliferation of
metal weapons and, in the longboat, the
development of a seacraft well suited to
raiding. Total war would very quickly
have been fatal to the communities of the
archipelago. Instead, it is likely that violence
was directed at the acquisition of animals,
movable wealth and perhaps also women.
The slotted spearhead was designed as a
thrusting weapon. The slots for which it is
named would have allowed for a secondary
shaft attachment using leather thongs or
similar, and would have made the spear
particularly effective for ship-to-shore
skirmishing, or perhaps even combat
between boat crews at sea.

Long dagger

c. 2750–1900 BCE

Copper alloy • Length: 17.1 cm (6¾ in.),
width: 4 cm (1½ in.) • Early Minoan II–
Middle Minoan IA • From Pseira, Crete

UNIVERSITY OF PENNSYLVANIA MUSEUM
OF ARCHAEOLOGY AND ANTHROPOLOGY,
PHILADELPHIA, USA

The final Neolithic settlement at Petras
Kephala currently offers the earliest evidence
for copper-smelting on Crete. The nature
of the operation at Chrysokamino on Crete
during this stage remains unclear, although
it was certainly involved in copper smelting
and the use of toxic arsenical alloying by
the late Early Bronze Age. The island of
Pseira is located off the north Cretan coast,
opposite Chrysokamino, and undoubtedly
formed one of its major markets. Daggers
such as this were a common product of
early metalworking facilities and would have
been prized by their owners as symbols of
both martial strength and access to a highly
valued new technology.

Female figurine

c. 6500–5800 BCE

Terracotta • Height: 18 cm (7 in.)
• Early Neolithic • From the 'shrine' at
Nea Nikomedeia, Macedonia, Greece

ARCHAEOLOGICAL MUSEUM OF
VEROIA, GREECE

Despite its name, the interpretation of
the so-called 'shrine' at Nea Nikomedeia is
far from clear. It contained an extraordinary
selection of material, including two
large greenstone axes, several hundred
unworked flint flakes and small clay
roundels of unknown function. It
also yielded five terracotta figurines,
including this one, which, like many
other Early Neolithic female figurines,
demonstrates a focus on the thighs
and buttocks (see page 46) and a rather
abstract modelling of facial features.
If the building was a shrine, then it is
possible to imagine such figures playing
a part in communal ritual, perhaps as
representations of goddesses, ancestors,
or symbols of fertility.

Kourotrophos figurine

c. 4800–4500 BCE
Terracotta • Height: 16.5 cm (6½ in.)
• Late Neolithic • From Sesklo, Thessaly, Greece
NATIONAL ARCHAEOLOGICAL MUSEUM,
ATHENS, GREECE

The motif of the kourotrophos or care-
giver (from the Greek kouros, meaning
'child' and trophos meaning 'rearer'
or 'nurse'), of which this is the earliest
Aegean example, survives into later Greek
history in the attributes of deities such
as Artemis, Demeter, Eileithyia and Gaia.
This figure may depict a Neolithic parallel,
though kourotrophoi encode themes of
motherhood, fertility, gender, sex,
protection and mortality, and other
interpretations are possible. The
infant perhaps wears a polos
cap, which in later periods
carries religious connotations.
The female was a composite
sculpture (acrolithic), her
head modelled separately
and inserted into a mortise
between the shoulders.
Multiple heads may have
been used for different
occasions or to represent
different individuals.

THE FAT LADY OF SALIAGOS

c. 5300–4500 BCE

Marble • Height: 5.9 cm (2¼ in.) • Late Neolithic • From Saliagos, off Antiparos, Cyclades
ARCHAEOLOGICAL MUSEUM OF PAROS, GREECE

The unflatteringly titled 'Fat Lady', heavily weathered and missing her head and right shoulder, is the oldest marble figurine known from the Cyclades. She derives from the Saliagos, today a small islet isolated between Greater Paros and Antiparos, though a promontory of the former during the Neolithic. It is the settlement here which lends its name to the first wave of permanent settlement into the Cycladic archipelago, and the culture thereof. Although the Cyclades had been visited regularly from at least the Upper Palaeolithic, the majority of these early trips appear to have been seasonal, directed toward the procurement of obsidian or the exploitation of annual tuna runs and other marine resources. By contrast, Late Neolithic colonists were primarily mixed farmers, turning to the sea – and particularly to tuna – to augment a diet which relied heavily on cereals and

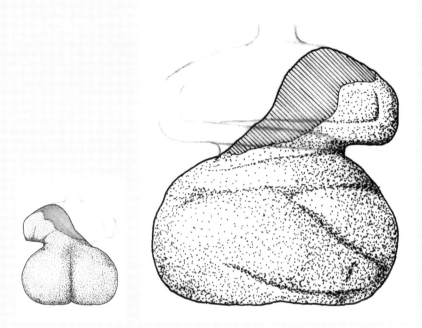

The 'fat lady' derives her name from her ample thighs and backside. She belongs to the 'steatopygous' class of Neolithic figurine and has parallels in marble from elsewhere in the Aegean.

domestic sheep and goat. They would have been forced to overcome a variety of difficulties, not least a scarcity of arable land, low levels of rainfall, a lack of potable water and parching summer winds. Larger islands such as Amorgos, Naxos, Paros, Siphnos and Thera offered the greatest chance of success, while marginal conditions elsewhere in the archipelago no doubt slowed the rate at which other settlements subsequently developed beyond

them. In this context, it is perhaps easier to understand the Fat Lady. Like other Neolithic figurines known from Crete and the Greek mainland, she demonstrates pronounced steatopygia, or fat accumulation around her thighs and buttocks. The ability to store fat offers an obvious benefit in societies where food shortages are a very real, and potentially fatal, reality, and may have become symbolically associated with fertility and fecundity.

Collared jar

c. 3100–2750 BCE

Marble • Height: 25.3 cm (10 in.), width 24.2 cm (9½ in.) • Early Cycladic I • Provenance unknown

BRITISH MUSEUM, LONDON, UK

Named for its resemblance to the lamps of the Greek Orthodox church, the kandila (collared jar) is the most common Early Cycladic I marble shape. Similar kandiles were manufactured in pottery, although versions in marble appear regularly as grave offerings, and were perhaps considered to be more appropriate for funerary use. Although their exact function is not clear, a ritual role seems likely. Holes drilled through vertical lugs on the body suggest they were closed with a lid, and chemical analyses have shown that some probably held alcohol.

Ring idol

c. 4300–3100 BCE

Gold • Height: 15.5 cm (6 in.), weight: 80.6 g (2¾ oz) • Final Neolithic • Provenance unknown

NATIONAL ARCHAEOLOGICAL MUSEUM, ATHENS, GREECE

Two relief nipples below the shank of this hammered sheet gold amulet make clear that it was intended as a schematic representation of the human form. The motif appears in Greece and the Balkans during the Neolithic period, and particularly at the extraordinarily gold-rich cemetery of Varna on the Black Sea coast of Bulgaria, clearly demonstrating contact between the two areas. The function of the amulets may have been to protect their wearers from evil, although their symbolism remains unclear. This example is, by far, the largest known.

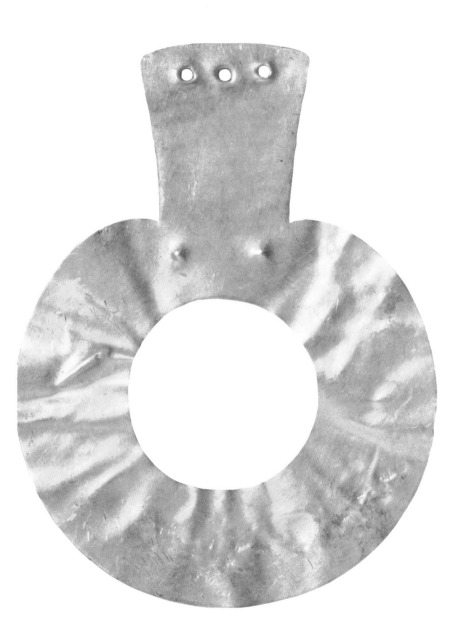

Sauceboat

c. 2750–2200 BCE
Gold • Height: 17 cm (6¾ in.) • Early Helladic II
• Provenance unknown (said to be from Heraia,
Arcadia, Greece)

LOUVRE, PARIS, FRANCE

The so-called sauceboat was first manufactured
during the Early Helladic II period and does not
survive in use beyond it. It is one of several shapes
that seem to attest to an increase in communal
feasting practices during a period in which
significant social developments are visible on
the Greek mainland. The shape is also known
in the Cyclades and as far west as the Anatolian
coast, and may well have been specifically
associated with the consumption of alcohol.
The asymmetric shape of ceramic examples is
sometimes thought to reflect its origin in other
materials. This is one of only two examples
known in gold.

The Goddess of Myrtos

c. 2400–2200 BCE

*Terracotta • Height: 21.5 cm (8½ in.), diameter
(maximum): 15.5 cm (6 in.) • Early Minoan IIB
• From Myrtos Fournou Koriphi, Crete*

ARCHAEOLOGICAL MUSEUM OF AGIOS
NIKOLAOS, CRETE, GREECE

The so-called Goddess of Myrtos is an elaborate
jug for which the small vessel being cradled by
the figure served as a spout. It was found fallen
from a small stone table in what appears to
have been the main room of a house, rather
than a shrine. Whether she truly represents
a goddess is not clear, although she may well
have had some symbolism, perhaps related to
the divine or the domestic, or simply to the
daily chore of retrieving water, historically
considered a female activity. She may have
been used publicly at communal feasts
within the modest Minoan settlement
of Myrtos Fournou Koriphi
or perhaps for rituals
within the household.

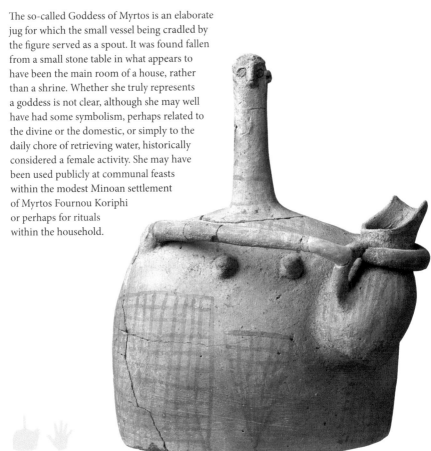

Monumental folded-arm figurine

c. 2750–2200 BCE

*Marble • Height: 1.5 m (5 ft) • Early
Cycladic II • Provenance unknown
(said to be from Amorgos, Cyclades)*

NATIONAL ARCHAEOLOGICAL MUSEUM,
ATHENS, GREECE

This monumental female is the largest
known example of a folded-arm figurine
and, with others of its type, represents the
earliest surviving monumental sculpture
from Greece. Its size suggests it may
have served as a cult figure although, like
its smaller counterparts, it could stand
unsupported and was reportedly found in
a grave, broken into pieces. Excavations
on Keros have uncovered a probable ritual
centre in which fragments of figurines and
other marble objects broken elsewhere
were systematically deposited. What this
practice represents is still unclear, although
a similar ideology may be evident here.

HARPIST AND
FLAUTIST FIGURINES

c. 2750–2200 BCE

Marble • Height of harpist: 29.5 cm (11½ in.), height of flautist: 20 cm (7¾ in.) • Early Cycladic II
• Provenance unknown (said to be from Keros, Cyclades)

METROPOLITAN MUSEUM OF ART, NEW YORK CITY, USA (HARPIST); NATIONAL
ARCHAEOLOGICAL MUSEUM, ATHENS, GREECE (FLAUTIST)

These figurines belong to a category of
'special' types displaying very different
motifs to those of the more common
female folded-arm varieties. While some
of these figurines are sexually ambiguous,
a majority are thought to represent males.
Examples include musicians such as the
flautist (right), shown here standing to play
the aulos or double flute, and the harpist
(opposite), a seated figure playing the
frame harp – an instrument with a frontal
ornament in the shape of a bird's bill that
has its origins in the Near East. Male figures
represent an extremely small proportion
of known marble sculpture and so it is
difficult to know what their function may
have been. While these examples probably
ended their use-life as grave offerings,
it is clear that the ways in which marble
figurines were perceived and utilized in
the Early Bronze Age archipelago were
potentially very complex. The motifs evident
here reflect common elite male activities,
although such actions also carry religious
overtones, and could perhaps have been
ritual in nature.

Alongside depictions of musicians, special figurine
types include men engaged in the act of raising
a toast or pouring a libation, and other multiple-
figure groups whose interpretation remains unclear.

Zoomorphic vessel

c. 2750–2200 BCE

Terracotta • Height: 10.8 cm (4¼ in.) • Early Cycladic II
• From Chalandriani, Syros, Cyclades

NATIONAL ARCHAEOLOGICAL MUSEUM,
ATHENS, GREECE

Holding forth and drinking from a bowl that opens
into its chest, this dark-on-light painted zoomorphic
figurine almost certainly represents a hedgehog,
although it is sometimes referred to as a bear. It
most likely possessed a ritual character, probably
associated with the pouring of libations. Hedgehogs
do not appear to have been considered particularly
significant animals in the Early Cycladic period;
the figure more generally reflects a trend towards
experimentation with animal-form vessels of various
types. A handful of parallels, perhaps depicting
hedgehogs, bears or pigs, are known from elsewhere
in the islands and at sites on the Greek mainland
with clear Cycladic connections, although they
remain extremely rare.

Complex and Monumental

The relieving triangle of the monumental Lion Gate at Mycenae is filled by a carved limestone slab depicting two lions whose front paws rest on a pair of altars supporting a central column. The motif may have been heraldic, perhaps the symbol of the royal house of Mycenae.

The earlier stages of the Middle Helladic have been considered a period of recession. Site numbers decreased as populations moved to form larger settlements. Trade networks remained relatively localized, although there are intermittent exceptions, and coastal sites benefited most from what little maritime trade there was. Burials were, generally, modest. Bioarchaeological analyses paint a rather grim picture of life for some of the population, with high rates of death during childhood, and high rates of malnutrition, stress fractures and malaria among those who survived. Against the relative poverty of the period, Kolonna on Aegina stands out. Having survived the disruption of the late Early Bronze Age unscathed, it developed into a major pottery production centre. Two small harbours provided access to maritime trade networks incorporating Crete, the Cyclades, Italy and Anatolia and, with substantial fortifications, monumental buildings and the earliest example of the 'warrior burial' of the type common during the Early Mycenaean period, represents an important antecedent of the mainland Mycenaean centres. In the Cyclades, trade resumed with

The Treasury of Atreus is the largest tholos tomb at Mycenae. Its total labour cost has been calculated at approximately 20,000 man days, and its inner lintel, approximately 120 tons, is the largest single block ever used by Mycenaean architects.

both Crete and the mainland, and important fortified settlements developed at sites like Ayia Irini on Kea and Phylakopi on Melos. A strong local identity is apparent across the archipelago, although material culture and architecture reflect an increasingly Minoan flavour later in the period as Minoan influence spread into the Aegean.

On Crete, the earlier Middle Bronze Age is characterized by the presence of monumental, court-centred complexes at sites such as Knossos, Malia, Phaistos and Petras. Once considered 'royal' centres with state-level political and economic authority, it is clear that their relationship with each other, and with other sites in their hinterland, was much more complex. Nevertheless, collectively they seem to have been substantial centres of consumption, and to a lesser degree storage, production and administration, as well as ceremonial activity, perhaps extended into the landscape through the peak sanctuaries that dotted the Cretan uplands from the Middle Minoan IA. The 'palatial' system, at least, was robust. Fire destructions at the end of the Middle Minoan II were followed by the reconstruction and reorganization of major centres on an even grander scale and the building of smaller 'palaces' elsewhere on the island. Large 'villa' buildings incorporating 'palatial' architectural features appeared in many lower towns, some perhaps home to an urban elite, others possibly administrative.

The Late Bronze Age saw unprecedented social and cultural change. On Crete, fire destructions during the Late Minoan IB prelude a serious reduction of Minoan influence in the Aegean. The cause remains unclear, although the super-colossal eruption of Thera (c. 1627–1600 BCE) should be implicated, even if indirectly. There is evidence for tsunami on the north Cretan coast, while the presence of pumice in a shrine at Nirou Chani suggests that the eruption was seen as a divine event. The 'palatial' complex at Knossos emerged out of this upheaval, perhaps to assume political and economic authority over much of Crete. Changes in material culture have been used to argue that Knossos was now under Mycenaean control. Whatever the reality, a Mycenaean presence seems certain from Late Minoan IIIA2 until its destruction.

Mycenaean culture developed in Crete's shadow among competing elites using disposable wealth to reinforce their status. This process culminated in *c.* 1420 BCE (Late Helladic IIIA) in the emergence of palaces at sites including Mycenae, Tiryns, Pylos, Agios Vasileios, Athens, Thebes, Orchomenos and Iolkos: monumental built spaces with 'cyclopean' fortifications, complexes of shrines and workshops, as well as a central megaron housing a throne room for the ruler (wanax). Monumental tholos tombs, visible earlier in the period, became the preserve of ruling elites and exemplified their ability to command labour and resources, as did major engineering projects at Pylos and Kopais. Palatial authority extended across substantial territories, while Mycenaean culture extended across the mainland as far north as Mount Olympus, eastwards to the Dodecanese and south to the Cyclades and Crete. Extensive trade networks connected the Mycenaean world with the Near East, Afghanistan, the Black Sea, the Balkans, Italy and Spain. Yet, for all its power and wealth, the palatial period lasted little over two centuries. Knossos was destroyed soon after *c.* 1300 BCE and by *c.* 1190 BCE the mainland palace system had also collapsed, inherent problems most likely rendering it unable to cope with external economic or environmental pressures.

The throne room at Knossos was almost certainly a cult space. The gypsum 'throne', perhaps occupied by a priestess rather than a king, was flanked by a fresco depicting a pair of wingless griffins. A sunken room known as a lustral basin lay opposite.

Grey Minyan goblet

c. 2050–1750 BCE

Ceramic • Diameter: 25.2 cm (9¾ in.) • Middle Helladic I–II
• From Mycenae, Argolid, Greece

BRITISH MUSEUM, LONDON, UK

Relatively little is known about the beginning of the Middle
Bronze Age on the Greek mainland; few settlements have been
excavated and most of our information comes from cemeteries.
Pottery provides key clues to the type of activities people were
engaged in and none is more characteristic of the period than
Grey Minyan. Named by Heinrich Schliemann for the legendary
King Minyas of Orchomenos, it was a fine tableware used for
feasting. This goblet would have been thrown on a fast wheel,
which enabled the potter to introduce sharp, carinated (ridged)
detail on the body, perhaps imitating similar vessels made of metal.

Hemispherical bowl with modelled figures

c. 1900–1850 BCE

Ceramic • Diameter at rim: 20 cm (7¾ in.) • Middle Minoan IB • From Tomb VII, Palaikastro, Crete

HERAKLION ARCHAEOLOGICAL MUSEUM, CRETE, GREECE

The interior of this bowl depicts a modelled shepherd accompanied by a ranked flock. Some 160 animals are preserved, although originally there may have been up to 200. The exterior is decorated with a red-and-white basketwork-style pattern that may have been intended to mimic the hurdle fencing of a stock fold. One of several bowls from Palaikastro that preserve modelled figures, it reflects the importance of weaving and wool production to the Middle Minoan economy. It was perhaps made for burial, or for use in rites designed to confer prosperity or to ensure the safety of the flock.

Kamares Ware krater with relief decoration

c. 1850–1700 BCE
Ceramic • Height: 45 cm (17¾ in.) • Middle Minoan II • From the palace at Phaistos, Crete
HERAKLION ARCHAEOLOGICAL MUSEUM, CRETE, GREECE

This krater reflects the demand for increasingly elaborate items of display during the Middle Bronze Age. It was found with a jug that had similar decoration and probably formed part of a larger drinking set. Modelling of this type is very rare and its meaning is not clear; often interpreted as lilies, the flowers do not actually correspond to a specific species. The design may simply have been used to distinguish its owner, or it is possible that the vessel was used to hold a ritual drink made with flowers. Although the decoration would have made it more difficult to use, the resulting symbolism must have been considered worthwhile. The theme is completed by painted petals on the rim and thorns or coral on the upper bowl and stem.

KAMARES WARE
BEAKED JUG

c. 1850–1675 BCE

Ceramic • Height: 27 cm (10½ in.) • Middle Minoan II–III • From Phaistos, Crete

HERAKLION ARCHAEOLOGICAL MUSEUM, CRETE, GREECE

Kamares Ware takes its name from the Kamares cave on the southern slope of Mount Ida, Crete, one of the most important Minoan rural sanctuaries and the site at which the style was first recognized in 1890. Kamares Ware appeared on Crete as the palace centres emerged, and it developed alongside them over the course of the Middle Bronze Age. Large volumes have been found at Knossos and Phaistos, although it is rare outside the palaces where it appears most often in ritual contexts. Minoan elites used participation in ritualized feasting, communal drinking and other public events to increase their social standing. Kamares was a high-status product and would have played an important role in realizing their ambitions. Characterized by elaborate decoration in red, white, yellow or orange on a dark background, its vibrant designs were intended to draw attention to its owner and its use conferred status. Access to a limited supply, or even control over its manufacture (as may have been the case at Knossos and Phaistos), would have been equally advantageous. Pottery of the 'Classical' Kamares style, to which this jug belongs, uses the widest range of colours and the greatest variety of motifs in the most complex combinations.

Situated at an altitude of 1,524 m (5,000 ft), the Kamares Cave represents the highest peak sanctuary known on Crete. It extended almost 100 m (328 ft) into the mountainside and witnessed cult activity throughout the Bronze Age.

House model

c. 1700–1675 BCE

Terracotta • Height: 18 cm (7 in.)
• Middle Minoan III • From
Archanes, Crete

HERAKLION ARCHAEOLOGICAL
MUSEUM, CRETE, GREECE

This model provides important evidence for Minoan architecture. Very few Bronze Age buildings survive above ground-floor level, although the design and ground plan is probably typical of a modest, mid-sized, Minoan town house, perhaps the home of a farmer or craftsperson. The ground floor includes a main room with a central column, hall, vestibule and porch, with a light well to provide light and air, while a staircase leads to a single upper-floor space with a projecting balcony and a flat roof (probably wooden, now lost) supported by piers and columns.

The Town Mosaic

c. 1700–1675 BCE
Faience • Dimensions: various
• Middle Minoan III • From the palace
at Knossos, Crete

HERAKLION ARCHAEOLOGICAL MUSEUM,
CRETE, GREECE

The Town Mosaic is made up of more
than fifty mould-made inlays of faience –
a glazed, non-clay ceramic, the main
ingredient of which is sand or quartz.
Faience was invented in Mesopotamia,
although the development of a later Minoan
faience industry is probably the result of
contact between Crete and Egypt, where the
material was extremely popular. More than
two dozen inlays depict building facades of
two and three storeys (right), which provide
important information on the appearance
of Minoan housing; others depict soldiers,
animals, trees and seawater. These pieces
would probably have been attached to an
item of wooden furniture and may have
formed a narrative, rather than a simply
decorative, scene.

Sealstone with Cretan Hieroglyphic script

c. 1850–1700 BCE

Green jasper • Length: 1.4 cm (½ in.), width: 1.1 cm (⅜ in.) • Middle Minoan II • Provenance unknown

BRITISH MUSEUM, LONDON, UK

The second-oldest Minoan writing system, Cretan Hieroglyphic appeared in *c.* 1800 BCE. It included at least ninety syllabograms (signs representing syllables) and thirty logograms (signs representing words), as well as signs for numerals and fractions. Fewer than 400 documents have been excavated and the script remains undeciphered. It was used by officials working in the emergent palatial economies of Crete, although where signs on sealstones accompanied naturalistic motifs, they may have functioned differently, carrying a symbolic value that conferred status on its owner.

The Phaistos Disc

c. 1700–1675 BCE

Terracotta • Diameter: 16.5 cm (6½ in.) • Middle Minoan III • From Phaistos, Crete

HERAKLION ARCHAEOLOGICAL MUSEUM, CRETE, GREECE

The enigmatic Phaistos Disc has no parallel. It is thought by some to be a religious text, but both the language and meaning of the disc remain unclear. Its two faces preserve a total of 241 symbols representing forty-five different pictographic signs, running from the edge to the centre within an incised spiral band. Further incisions define individual groups of signs, perhaps representing single words. Incredibly, these signs were impressed using individual metal stamps, as in modern typography. Such stamps would probably have been used repeatedly, raising the possibility that other discs remain to be discovered.

LINEAR B TABLETS

c. 1330–1190 BCE

Clay • Length (Tripod Tablet, centre): 26.5 cm (10½ in.), widths (PY Ta 709–712, top): 25 cm (9 ¾ in.) and (PY Eq 213, bottom): 18 cm (7 in.) • Late Helladic IIIB • From the Palace of Nestor at Pylos, Greece

NATIONAL ARCHAEOLOGICAL MUSEUM, ATHENS, GREECE

'B' SYLLABARY PHONETIC 'GRID'   Fig. 1 MGFV

1: State as at 28 Jan 51 before publication of Pylos inscriptions

CONSONANTS	Vowel 1 (NIL?) (-o ?) * typical 'nominative' of nouns which change their last theme syllable in oblique cases	Vowel 2 -i ? * typical changed last syllable before -ι and -B.	Other vowels? -a, -e, -u ? * changes in last syllable caused by other endings (5 vowels in oil, rather than 4 ?)	Doubtful
1 t- ?	ag	aj	ah / ol	ax (Sundwall)
2 r- ??	az	iw	ol	
3 s- ??	eg	aw	oc / oj	
4 n- ?? / s- ??	od	ok	ib e-	is / oh
5		ak	e²	
6 l- ?	ac	ij		
7 h- ??	ix		ia	
8 θ- ??	en		ia	rr
9 m- ? / k- ??	ay if an enclitic 'and'		al	al
10				om / av
11				
12				

The syllabic Linear B script owes its identification as an archaic form of Greek to a brilliant young linguist and architect, Michael Ventris. Announcing his discovery via a legendary BBC radio broadcast on 1 July 1952, he subsequently worked with a young Cambridge scholar, John Chadwick, to tackle the corpus of now-decipherable documents. On 6 September 1956, weeks after the results of this collaboration were published, Ventris was killed in a road accident, aged thirty-four.

The majority of the more than 5,000 tablets currently known come from Knossos and Pylos, where they were copied out by palatial scribes whose individual hands can now be recognized. All are accidental survivals, baked hard when the archives in which they were stored were destroyed by fire. They refer to activities in a single year. Texts include rosters and rations; inventories of agricultural commodities, raw materials and manufactured goods; obligations; and the personal names and roles of thousands of individuals employed by or subject to the palaces. The tablets offer an unparalleled wealth of information on Mycenaean society, politics, religion and economy.

Ventris (pictured) was ultimately responsible for the decipherment, but was guided by the insights of other scholars including Emmett L. Bennett and Alice Kober.

Kylix

c. 1315–1190 BCE

Ceramic • Height: 19.6 cm (7¾ in.),
diameter at rim: 17.1 cm (6¾ in.) • Late Helladic
IIIB • From Zygouries, near Corinth, Greece

METROPOLITAN MUSEUM
OF ART, NEW YORK CITY, USA

The rise of the Mycenaean palaces, and the
consolidation of power in the hands of
their ruling elites, brought a new level
of social and economic stability to the
Greek mainland and saw the emergence
of a common Mycenaean culture across
much of the Aegean. As a result, pottery
became more uniform and travelled across
far greater distances, with exports identified
as far west as Spain and at least as far east
as Syria. Mass-produced and of very high
quality, the wheel-made wine cup known
as the kylix appeared in *c.* 1420 BCE and
quickly became extremely popular. This
example is slightly later in date and has
been decorated with a stylized flower.

Oxhide ingot

c. 1410–1190 BCE

Copper • Length: 35 cm (13¾ in.), width:
22 cm (8¾ in.), weight: 9.9 kg (21¾ lb) • Late
Helladic IIIA–B • From Kyme, Euboea, Greece

NUMISMATIC MUSEUM, ATHENS, GREECE

This ingot is one of a group of nineteen
that made up part of the cargo of a Late
Bronze Age merchant ship sunk at Kyme
Bay, off the island of Euboea. It is of the
so-called 'oxhide' type, named for its broad
resemblance to the skin. It was in this form
(and to a lesser degree as rounded 'bun'
ingots) that raw copper was transported
across the Late Bronze Age Aegean. Very
substantial cargos of similar ingots have
been identified from wrecks at Cape
Gelidonya (approx. 1 ton) and Ulu Burun
(approx. 10 tons in total, with a further ton
of tin ingots), off the Anatolian coast.

Storage jar

c. 1460–1370 BCE
*Ceramic • Height: 1.1 m (3½ ft),
diameter at rim: 0.7 m (2¼ ft) • Late
Minoan II–IIIA1 • From the palace at
Knossos, Crete*

BRITISH MUSEUM, LONDON, UK

Large pithoi were vital to the
Bronze Age agricultural
economy. Used for the long-term
storage of dry foodstuffs, wine
and olive oil, they ensured food
supply over winter, offered
protection against crop failure
and provided opportunity to
accumulate agricultural surplus
for sale or redistribution at
public events. This example was
recovered from the West
Magazine at Knossos, a series
of eighteen rooms capable of
storing 420 pithoi with a total
capacity of about 231,000 litres
(61,000 gal). Incised bands on
the body imitate rope, while
heavy handles allowed the vessel
to be manoeuvred and its
contents decanted.

Inscribed stirrup jar

c. 1315–1190 BCE
Ceramic • Height: 44.5 cm
(17½ in.) • Late Helladic IIIB •
From the Kadmeia, Thebes, Greece

ARCHAEOLOGICAL MUSEUM
OF THEBES, GREECE

Named for the shape of its handle, the stirrup jar was used to hold valuable liquids such as oil and wine, possessing a small mouth and high neck to prevent spillage and minimize loss. This example belongs to a rare group, found in quantity at Thebes, which preserve painted Linear B syllabograms on the body. They refer to a man ('a-re-zo-me-ne') and a settlement in western Crete, perhaps the manufacturer of the vessel's contents and its origin. A single jar may have served as a label for a larger shipment. The original purpose of the inscription was communication and administration; in reuse, however, it may have conferred additional value on the vessel itself.

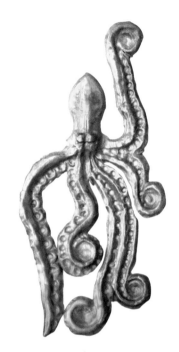

Gold-foil ornaments

c. 1675–1600 BCE

*Gold • Height of octopus (top): 10 cm
(4 in.), sphinx: 2.5 cm (1 in.), octopus
(bottom): 3.1 cm (1¼ in.) • Late Helladic I
• From Shaft Grave III, Grave Circle A,
Mycenae, Argolid, Greece*

NATIONAL ARCHAEOLOGICAL
MUSEUM, ATHENS, GREECE

An extraordinary array of gold-foil
cut-outs was recovered from Shaft Grave
III. Those with perforations were sewn on
to the burial shroud; those without may
have been glued or simply placed. Motifs
include divinities and animals, both real
and mythical, in a variety of poses and
arrangements. Some are clearly derived
from Minoan art and each was most likely
chosen for its symbolic association to
death and the divine. The sphinx was
considered a guardian, while the octopus,
with its ability to regrow tentacles, perhaps
served as a metaphor for regeneration.
This association may explain why the
animal is sometimes depicted with less
than its full complement of eight limbs.

The Bee Pendant

c. 1700–1600 BCE
*Gold • Width: 4.6 cm (1¾ in.) • Middle Minoan III–
Late Minoan IA • From the Chrysolakkos (gold pit)
complex at Malia, Crete*

HERAKLION ARCHAEOLOGICAL MUSEUM,
CRETE, GREECE

The famous bee pendant from Malia incorporates
a variety of complex gold-working techniques
including repoussé, filigree and granulation,
and offers some idea of the technical and artistic
skill of goldsmiths working on Crete during
the Protopalatial period. The pendant depicts
opposing bees supporting a drop of honey (or
perhaps a pollen ball) elaborated with pendant
discs at the wings and stings, and a filigree cage
with a small gold sphere (of unknown meaning)
above their heads.

Duck vase

c. 1700–1600 BCE
Rock crystal • Length: 13.2 cm
(5¼ in.), height: 5.7 cm (2¼ in.) •
Middle Helladic III–Late Helladic I
• From Grave Omicron, Grave Circle
B, Mycenae, Argolid, Greece

NATIONAL ARCHAEOLOGICAL
MUSEUM, ATHENS, GREECE

Carved from a single piece of rock crystal (colourless quartz), this exquisite spouted bowl takes the form of a duck in a typical Egyptian pose, but was probably imported to Mycenae from a lapidary workshop on Crete. Minoan craftsmen more commonly incorporated rock crystal into small items of jewelry, and only very rarely utilized it for larger vessels given its exceptional hardness and the technical difficulties it presented. This would have been a very high-value object and may have formed the subject of a diplomatic gift exchange between Minoan rulers on Crete and an emerging Mycenaean elite, one of whom, perhaps, chose it to accompany her to the grave.

The Lion Hunt Dagger

c. 1675–1600 BCE
Bronze, gold, silver and niello • Length:
23.7 cm (9¼ in.) • Late Helladic I • From
Shaft Grave IV, Grave Circle A, Mycenae,
Argolid, Greece

NATIONAL ARCHAEOLOGICAL
MUSEUM, ATHENS, GREECE

A celebrated example of Mycenaean
art, this bronze dagger was intended
for display rather than battle. It depicts
heavy spearmen and a lone archer
moving on a lion that has already felled
one of their party. On the overside, a
lion downs a deer as the surviving mob
takes flight. These scenes were produced
using techniques known as 'painting in
metal' or 'metallmalerei'. Incised metal
elements were fixed, and hidden, on the
blade using niello (a mix of copper, lead
and silver sulphides). Once cooled, they
were carefully exposed, with niello in
the incisions providing detail. Lion art
is unusually common in Grave Circle A.
Symbolizing strength and power, it may
have been deliberately chosen to reflect
the authority of its occupants.

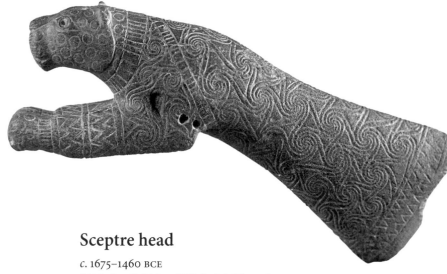

Sceptre head

c. 1675–1460 BCE

Schist • Length: 14.8 cm (5¾ in.) • Late Minoan I
• From the palace at Malia, Crete

HERAKLION ARCHAEOLOGICAL MUSEUM,
CRETE, GREECE

This unique sceptre head was excavated from
a possible ritual space and seems certain to
be ceremonial, but how it was used, and who
wielded it, is not clear. The butt takes the form
of a leopard in a flying gallop – a common pose
for animals in Minoan art – whereas the rear
takes the form of a double axe in a deliberate
combination of two potent symbols of power.
The eyes of the leopard would have been inlaid,
and attachment holes for additional inlays can
be seen at the shoulder. A variety of abstract
motifs cover the body of the animal, although
incised bands across the chest and neck perhaps
represent a harness.

The Toreador Fresco

c. 1675–1460 BCE

Lime plaster • Height: 0.8 m (2½ ft), width: 1 m (3¼ ft)
• Middle Minoan III–Late Minoan I • From the palace
at Knossos, Crete

HERAKLION ARCHAEOLOGICAL MUSEUM,
CRETE, GREECE

Part of a five-panel composition, the iconic Toreador
Fresco depicts an acrobat at the back of a charging bull.
A second figure prepares to leap, while a third waits with
arms outstretched. The event may have resembled the
Course Landaise of modern southwest France. Bulls
feature centrally in Knossian iconography and may
have acted as a symbol of Knossian power. The central
court may have served as an arena for bull-sports,
although it was barely large enough. It is possible that
the later myth of Theseus and the Minotaur preserves
a corrupted memory of Bronze Age athletes proving
themselves against bulls at the palace.

The Vapheio Cups

c. 1675–1410 BCE
Gold • Height: 7.8 cm (3 in.), diameter: 10.7 cm (4¼ in.)
• Late Helladic I–II • From Vapheio Tholos, Laconia, Greece
NATIONAL ARCHAEOLOGICAL MUSEUM,
ATHENS, GREECE

Monumental tholos tombs appeared on the Greek
mainland during the late Middle Bronze Age against a
backdrop of political competition between Mycenaean
elites. Intended as a conspicuous statement of power,
their visibility in the landscape made them a target for
looters. Like most, the Vapheio Tholos was robbed,
although these cups survived in a cist (slab-lined pit)
below the main chamber floor. Perhaps manufactured
by a Minoan goldsmith, both depict scenes of bull
capture in repoussé. The first shows a youth calmly
roping a bull while it mates, with three bulls grazing
nearby; the second depicts a bull caught in a net hung
between two olive trees, while another attacks a group
of hunters.

Acrobat

c. 1700–1460 BCE

*Ivory • Length: 29.5 cm (11½ in.) • Middle Minoan III–
Late Minoan I • From the palace at Knossos, Crete*

HERAKLION ARCHAEOLOGICAL MUSEUM,
CRETE, GREECE

This spectacular ivory depicts an acrobat in
flight. Like the Toreador Fresco (see page 83), it
once adorned an upper-floor room in the east
wing at Knossos, perhaps even a loggia in which
bull-sports were showcased. Associated ivory
fragments, including at least two other figures,
suggest that it formed part of a larger composition.
The acrobat, arms outstretched and body taut,
was manufactured in sections and joined using
dowels and tenons. The right arm and leg, as well
as the waist, have been lost, although the surviving
anatomical detail of musculature, veins and even
fingernails is exceptional. A gilt-bronze hairpiece
once adorned the head and a gold codpiece was
probably attached at the waist.

Sealstones with naturalistic motifs

c. 1675–1370 BCE

Steatite (octopus), agate (Mistress of Animals), carnelian (bulls), haematite (lion/cattle) • Length (range): Octopus 2 cm (¾ in.)–Mistress of Animals 3.5 cm (1½ in.) • Late Minoan I/II–IIIA1 • From Knossos, Greece

HERAKLION ARCHAEOLOGICAL MUSEUM, CRETE, GREECE

The Middle Bronze Age adoption of the Near Eastern horizontal bow lathe on Crete enabled lapidaries to manufacture seals from hard, semi-precious stones and revolutionized Minoan glyptic (engraved) art. Decorated with combinations of abstract and naturalistic motifs, these seals were drilled, threaded and worn as bracelets or pendants. Loaded with symbolism, seals could transmit the rank, social affiliations or identity of their owners. They were used administratively to identify or secure property, although some may have been worn for protection or simply appreciated as jewelry.

Lyre

c. 1315–1190 BCE

Ivory • Length of right arm (preserved): 27 cm (10½ in.), as reconstructed: 50 cm (19¾ in.), perhaps originally: 60–75 cm (23½–29½ in.) • Late Helladic IIIB • From the Menidi Tholos, Attica, Greece

NATIONAL ARCHAEOLOGICAL MUSEUM, ATHENS, GREECE

Although well attested in Bronze Age art, surviving examples of prehistoric instruments are few. Sistra (rattles) and hand cymbals are known from Crete, while an ivory aulos (flute) is known from Mycenae. The chelys lyre, which utilizes a tortoiseshell for the sound box, has been identified at Phylakopi. This elaborately carved lyre is of a type known as the phorminx, which would have been held in the crook of the left arm and plucked or strummed with the right hand. It has been incorrectly restored using an ivory plaque from a box or footstool as a sound box. The Pylos Bard Fresco and Aghia Triadha Sarcophagus (see pages 96 and 124) offer some idea of its original appearance.

The Priest King

c. 1675–1460 BCE
Lime plaster • Length: 2.1 m (6¾ ft) • Late Minoan I
• From the palace at Knossos, Crete

HERAKLION ARCHAEOLOGICAL MUSEUM,
CRETE, GREECE

Also known as the Prince of the Lilies, this painted
stucco relief, as it appears today, is the result of heavy
restoration undertaken in 1905 by Swiss artist Emile
Gilliéron Jnr, at the request of Arthur Evans. Imagined
as a monumental, long-haired male wearing a kilt
and codpiece, a crown of feathers and lilies and a lily
necklace, the reconstruction remains contentious. It
has been suggested that Gilliéron's version combines
fragments from a number of different figures, and
several alternative interpretations have been offered.
While his identity, his pose and the scene in which he
featured remain unclear, the rope he carries is a total
fabrication – an addition to support Evans's theory
that the 'Priest King' originally led a sacred animal.

THE MINIATURE FRIEZE

c. 1675–1600 BCE

Lime plaster • Height: 20–40 cm (7¾–15¾ in.) • Late Cycladic I
• From the West House at Akrotiri, Thera (Santorini)

NATIONAL ARCHAEOLOGICAL MUSEUM, ATHENS, GREECE

Victim to the Late Bronze Age eruption of Thera, Akrotiri was buried beneath metres of volcanic tephra, resulting in an extraordinary degree of preservation and a unique insight into life in a prehistoric Cycladic town. Surviving in places to second-floor level, the West House is one of Akrotiri's best-understood buildings. The ground floor served for storage and household crafts, while upper-floor rooms were residential. Among them, room 5 was one of the most richly decorated in the settlement. The Miniature Frieze extended across three of its four walls. The east wall was decorated with a 'Nilotic' landscape, including palms, papyrus plants, birds and

griffin. The south wall depicted a nautical procession between two towns, perhaps undertaken as part of a religious festival, and watched by men and women from windows, rooftops and the shore. These towns may well have been Theran, and it is possible that one may represent Akrotiri itself. The north wall depicted a naval engagement in which sailors in 'Aegean' kilts appear victorious over a naked enemy. Soldiers armed with oxhide shields and boar's tusk helmets may be allied warriors marching ashore in triumph. At the top of the scene, stockherds drive their animals into an enclosure while robed figures perform a possible religious ritual known as 'the ceremony on the hill'.

The scenes that decorated the north wall of room 5 are highly complex and their fragmentary nature makes interpretation difficult. It is possible that the drowning figures shown here have been vanquished, although they may represent the victims of a shipwreck.

Pyxis

c. 1410–1315 BCE
*Ivory • Height: 16 cm (6¼ in.), diameter:
11 cm (4¼ in.) • Late Helladic IIIA • From the
Athenian Agora, Greece*

MUSEUM OF THE ANCIENT AGORA,
ATHENS, GREECE

Found in the most impressive Mycenaean tomb in the Agora, this tin-lined pyxis is unparalleled in its execution. Made from a single imported tusk, it likely held cosmetics. The lid depicts a griffin mauling a pair of deer, and the body a pair of griffin flanking a mob of four. The first of the pair has its kill, while the second strikes an agonized stag, bending a tree beneath the downdraught of its wings. The Minoan character of the design suggests a link with Crete during a period when the island appears to be under Mycenaean control.

The Boar Hunt Fresco

c. 1315–1190 BCE
*Lime plaster • Height: 35.5 cm (14 in.) • Late
Helladic IIIB • From Tiryns, Argolid, Greece*

NATIONAL ARCHAEOLOGICAL MUSEUM,
ATHENS, GREECE

The Boar Hunt fresco was recovered from an architectural dump on the west slope of the acropolis at Tiryns, although it would not have been out of place in the palace megaron. Hunting was a popular elite activity, and with the boar as prey the sport may have carried an additional ideological or ritual significance. The depiction of female charioteers is unusual and, while the pair appear to be spectators, Linear B texts make clear that women held specified roles associated with the hunt. These figures are part of a much larger scene depicting spearmen and a dog pack downing a boar.

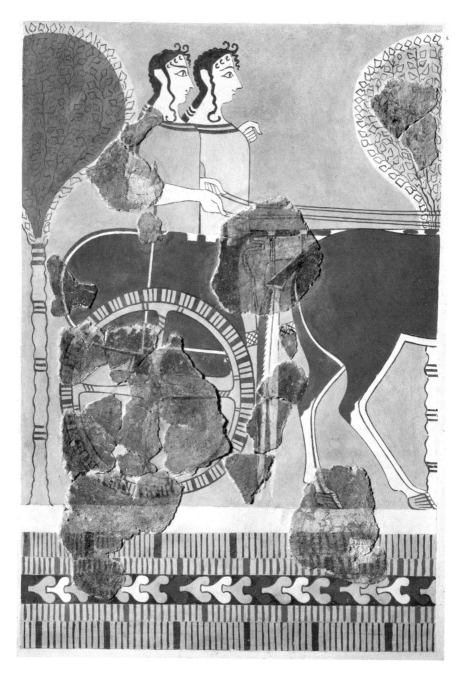

THE PYLOS BARD FRESCO

c. 1315–1190 BCE

Lime plaster • Height: 61 cm (24 in.) • Late Helladic IIIB • From the throne room of the palace at Pylos, Messenia, Greece

ARCHAEOLOGICAL MUSEUM OF CHORA TRIFYLIA, MESSENIA, GREECE

The throne room at Pylos measured almost 145 m² (1,560 ft²). A huge, brightly painted ceremonial hearth lay at its centre. It was framed by four wooden columns, which supported a clerestory above. At the northeast wall stood the throne, probably made of wood and spectacularly inlaid. A huge octopus decorated the floor beyond, while vibrantly painted panels covered the remainder. Spectacular frescoes reflected power and authority. Deer and papyrus adorned the southwest wall and griffins and lions flanked the throne; a feasting scene decorated the same wall nearby, while the 'Pylos Bard' adorned the east corner. It depicts a robed figure atop a vividly coloured rock. He holds a lyre; a bird or griffin may represent the last of his words taking flight. Some scholars have suggested that the figure represents the mythical Orpheus, chief among poets and musicians, who was capable of charming animals into dance.

The throne room of a Mycenaean palace lay at its centre in a complex known as a megaron. Comprising porch, vestibule and main hall, its decoration conveyed social and political messages to visiting dignitaries.

Chariot model

c. 1315–1190 BCE
*Terracotta • Length: 32 cm (12½ in.), height: 18.5 cm
(7¼ in.) • Late Helladic IIIB • From a tomb at Megalo
Monastiri, Thessaly, Greece*

ARCHAEOLOGICAL MUSEUM OF VOLOS, GREECE

Both complete chariots and constituent parts are
well attested in Linear B records. However, while a
handful of paired-horse burials probably represent
chariot teams and bronze fittings are occasionally
identified, no chariot frames have survived.
Artistic representations are therefore invaluable
for understanding their design and function. This
model depicts a quadrant chariot. With a cab
formed of hide over a wooden frame, it was light,
fast and low to the ground, although it is not clear
how such vehicles operated in the throng of battle.

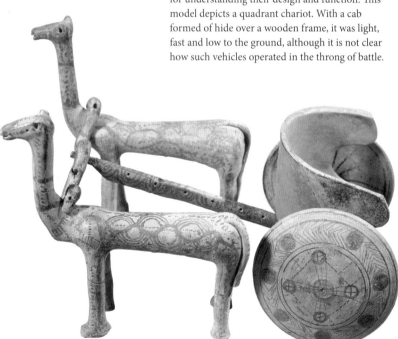

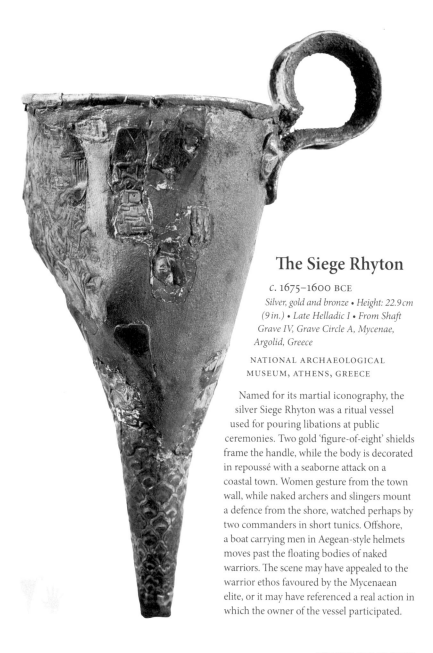

The Siege Rhyton

c. 1675–1600 BCE

*Silver, gold and bronze • Height: 22.9 cm
(9 in.) • Late Helladic I • From Shaft
Grave IV, Grave Circle A, Mycenae,
Argolid, Greece*

NATIONAL ARCHAEOLOGICAL
MUSEUM, ATHENS, GREECE

Named for its martial iconography, the
silver Siege Rhyton was a ritual vessel
used for pouring libations at public
ceremonies. Two gold 'figure-of-eight' shields
frame the handle, while the body is decorated
in repoussé with a seaborne attack on a
coastal town. Women gesture from the town
wall, while naked archers and slingers mount
a defence from the shore, watched perhaps by
two commanders in short tunics. Offshore,
a boat carrying men in Aegean-style helmets
moves past the floating bodies of naked
warriors. The scene may have appealed to the
warrior ethos favoured by the Mycenaean
elite, or it may have referenced a real action in
which the owner of the vessel participated.

Boar's tusk helmet

c. 1315–1190 BCE

Boar's tusk • Height (reconstructed): 30 cm (11¾ in.)
• Late Helladic IIIB • From Chamber Tomb 515 at
Mycenae, Argolid, Greece

NATIONAL ARCHAEOLOGICAL
MUSEUM, ATHENS, GREECE

In Homer's epic poem the *Iliad*, Odysseus
received a boar's tusk helmet from Meriones,
captain of one of the eighty Cretan ships sent
against Troy. The description is so detailed it
probably represents Bronze Age knowledge,
preserved through oral histories or sung epic.
This helmet was formed of tusk plates, drilled
and bound in close rows to a cap of felt or
leather. Although not that robust, it was perhaps
an insignia of rank and a demonstration of
the wearer's skill as a hunter. The double hook
on this example suggests elaboration with a
plume or crest.

Grave stele

c. 1675–1600 BCE

Poros limestone • Height (preserved): 1.3 m (4¼ ft), width: 1 m (3¼ ft) • Late
Helladic I • From Shaft Grave V, Grave Circle A, Mycenae, Argolid, Greece

NATIONAL ARCHAEOLOGICAL MUSEUM, ATHENS, GREECE

Fifteen adults, one adolescent and a child were buried in the six shaft
graves of Grave Circle A, suggesting that each of the seventeen stelae
recovered there commemorated a specific individual. This group
is the earliest large-scale relief sculpture from the Greek mainland,
representing a new form of memorial for a new and powerful elite.
This example depicts a warrior (perhaps the deceased) in a box
chariot, reaching for his sword and driving his horse towards a nude
figure, who, with weapon raised, may represent a vanquished enemy.
This may be a reference to a real event, or simply a suitably elite motif.

THE DENDRA PANOPLY

c. 1410–1315 BCE

Bronze • Dimensions: unknown • Late Helladic IIIA • From a tomb at Dendra, Argolid, Greece

ARCHAEOLOGICAL MUSEUM OF NAFPLION, GREECE

This complete bronze corslet represents the earliest surviving full-body armour in Europe. Weighing less than 15 kg (33 lb), it is formed of fifteen separate sections, including bronze plates (1–1.5 mm thick) to protect the body, pauldrons to protect the shoulders and a high gorget to protect the neck. Traces of a leather lining still survive in places. A single bronze greave (shin guard) and a helmet made of boar's tusk were recovered in the same tomb. Once thought to have been too cumbersome to be practicable on the battlefield, or at best suitable only for heavy troops fighting from chariots, recent experiments with a modern reproduction of the suit have proven it to be surprisingly effective, both in terms of mobility and the protection it affords, suggesting that it may have been worn by heavy infantry armed with swords or spears. Corslets of this type appear as ideograms in Linear B, while at Pylos, the term 'o-pa-wo-ta' may refer to individual sections of plate. Such corslets may have been fairly common among elite Mycenaean soldiers, although isolated fragments of fewer than ten examples are known. It is likely that many warriors would have worn cheaper, lighter armour made of organic materials, including leather and linen, that have not survived.

The Dendra panoply is uniquely complete, although other fragments of Mycenaean bronze armour are known. This pauldron (shoulder guard) from Tomb 8 at Dendra may have been attached to a linen corslet, or it may have been buried in lieu of a full suit.

Kernos

c. 2200–1850 BCE
Ceramic • Height: 34.6 cm (13¾ in.),
diameter: 35.5 cm (14 in.) • Early Cycladic III–
Middle Cycladic I • Provenance unknown (said to
be from Melos, Greece)

METROPOLITAN MUSEUM OF ART,
NEW YORK CITY, USA

The kernos was a ritual vessel, with each of
its twenty-five flasks and the central bowl
probably used to hold offerings of foodstuffs,
including seeds, grains, fruit and drink. This
large, simply decorated example on a high
foot is one of three vessels said to have been
found on the Cycladic island of Melos in
1829 by Captain Richard Copeland of HMS
Mastiff, during his five-year survey of the
waters around Greece and Italy. It is likely
that the group, which included a jug and
jar, came from the same tomb, and perhaps
from the major settlement of Phylakopi on
the north coast of the island.

Votive figurine

c. 2200–1850 BCE

Terracotta • Height: 15 cm (6 in.) • Early Minoan III–Middle Minoan I • From the peak sanctuary of Petsophas, near Palaikastro, Crete

HERAKLION ARCHAEOLOGICAL MUSEUM, CRETE, GREECE

Peak sanctuaries were established across Crete at the beginning of the Middle Bronze Age, although the tradition may be Neolithic. Established on high summits, perhaps initially by shepherds utilizing upland pasture, they were the locations for communal cults directed towards multiple deities. Rituals commonly took place in the open air and were characterized by feasting and the deposition of votives into natural features in the bedrock. This armed youth holds his arms in the typical pose of an adorant and may have been an offering to Zeus.

Psi, Tau and Phi figurines

c. 1410–1190 BCE

Terracotta • Heights (Psi): 11.5 cm (4½ in.), (Tau): 10 cm (4 in.), (Phi): 8 cm (3¼ in.) • Late Helladic IIIA–B • Provenance unknown (Tau and Psi, said to be from Athens, Greece; Phi said to be from Melos, Cyclades, Greece).

BRITISH MUSEUM,
LONDON, UK

The handmade female figurines known as Psi, Tau and Phi are named for the similarity of their respective poses to the Greek letters: Ψ, T Φ. They are highly stylized, with clothing suggested by vertical painted lines and features modelled in the most basic way. These figurines were produced en masse and have been recovered in their thousands from a range of contexts in settlements and cemeteries. They may have served as inexpensive religious icons, or perhaps children's toys. Their function may have been interchangeable over time or in different regions according to local custom.

Gold leaf from
the body of an infant

c. 1675–1600 BCE

*Gold • Total estimated length 60 cm (24 in.) • Late Helladic I
• From Grave III, Grave Circle A, Mycenae, Argolid, Greece*

NATIONAL ARCHAEOLOGICAL MUSEUM, ATHENS, GREECE

Although the body of this infant no longer survives, the gold
leaf used to dress it for burial has preserved poignant details,
such as fingers, toes and pierced ears. The unique nature of
this treatment, as well as the care taken and cost involved,
suggests that the child was heir to a position of considerable,
perhaps even royal, authority. The body was laid to rest
on the chest of a middle-aged woman, perhaps the child's
mother, who wore a large perishable crown and who was of
exceptionally high, possibly religious, rank in her own right.

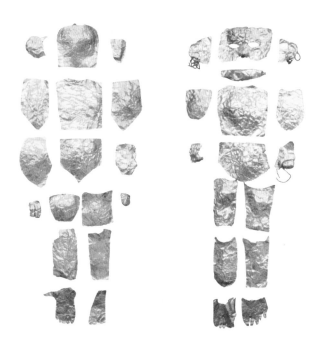

Miniature labrys

c. 1700–1460 BCE

Gold • Dimensions: unknown • Middle Minoan III–Late Minoan I • From the Arkalochori Cave, Crete

HERAKLION ARCHAEOLOGICAL
MUSEUM, CRETE, GREECE

The cave of Arkalochori is located about 3 km (1¾ miles) south of the Minoan palace at Galatas and has yielded the largest assemblage of votive material of any Minoan cave sanctuary on Crete. A collection of bronze objects weighing more than 18 Turkish okas (22.5 kg/50 lb) was reportedly retrieved from the cave by locals and sold as scrap before the first systematic excavations in 1912. Among the incredible array of votive objects recovered since are some thirty gold double axes, or labrys, a religious symbol in the same manner as the Christian cross.

THE MASK OF AGAMEMNON

c. 1675–1600 BCE

Gold • Height: 25 cm (9¾ in.), width: 27 cm (10½ in.),
weight: 169 g (6 oz) • Late Helladic I • From Shaft Grave V,
Grave Circle A, Mycenae, Argolid, Greece

NATIONAL ARCHAEOLOGICAL MUSEUM,
ATHENS, GREECE

The Mask of Agamemnon is arguably the most iconic object of
the Aegean Bronze Age. Named by Heinrich Schliemann for the
Mycenaean ruler of Homer's *Iliad*, it is the most accomplished
of five masks from Grave Circle A. The mask would have been
secured to the face of the deceased with cord threaded through
holes below each ear. At least five adults, one adolescent and
an infant were buried in Grave V. The owner of the mask, a
muscular man approximately twenty-five years old, was perhaps
the last. His age suggests a sudden or violent death, although
his only discernible injuries are a wound or stress fracture on
the right leg and a compression fracture on the spine, neither
of which would necessarily have been fatal. He was buried with
a variety of other goods including gilt-bronze weapons, a gold
breastplate decorated with repoussé spirals, a necklace with
eagle decoration and a gold rosette armband. Scientific analysis
has raised the possibility that he was not local to Mycenae or,
at least, that his diet was rich in non-local foodstuffs.

*The offerings of Grave
Circle A far exceed those
of Grave Circle B in wealth
and craftsmanship. In
c. 1250 BCE, the circle was
renovated and brought
within the fortification wall,
perhaps out of respect or to
help Mycenae's then-rulers
legitimize their power.*

Rhyton

c. 1675–1460 BCE
*Rock crystal • Height: 16 cm
(6¼ in.) • Late Minoan I • From
the palace treasury at Zakros, Crete*

HERAKLION ARCHAEOLOGICAL
MUSEUM, CRETE, GREECE

Carved from a single block of rock
crystal, this ritual rhyton is testament
to the skill of the Minoan lapidary, who
would have roughed it out using fine
bronze chisels, drilled and then,
slowly and with extreme care,
finished the vase inside and out
using emery, aware that even the
most minor fault would have caused
it to crack. The neck ring is formed
of separate C-shaped rock crystal
pieces secured by gilt-faience
bands, while the handle is formed
of fourteen rock crystal beads,
each drilled and threaded with
bronze wire. This vessel was
probably a special commission,
the exceptional effort involved in
its manufacture adding to both its
value and the status of its owner.

The Grandstand Fresco

c. 1675–1460 BCE
Lime plaster • Height (without border): 26 cm (10¼ in.)
• Late Minoan I • From the palace at Knossos, Crete
HERAKLION ARCHAEOLOGICAL MUSEUM,
CRETE, GREECE

At the centre of the Grandstand Fresco is a tripartite (three-part) shrine overlooking a central court. Groups of priestesses sit at either side – their size and elaborate dress signify their importance. Rows of smaller women stand to the left and right, while others watch from porticoes at first-floor level. A small number of white females stand in the court itself, almost lost amid ranks of anonymous males. Given the focus on females, the scene may memorialize a public rite of passage undertaken within the central palace sanctuary at Knossos by local girls entering womanhood.

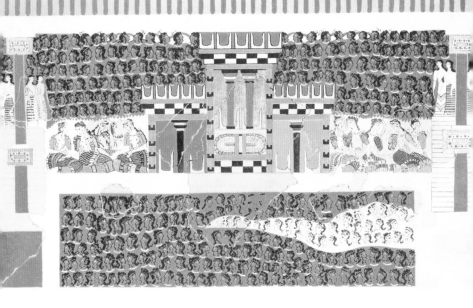

The Boxer Rhyton

c. 1675–1460 BCE

Serpentinite • Height (restored): 44.8 cm
(17½ in.) • Late Minoan I • From the royal
villa at Aghia Triadha, near Phaistos, Crete

HERAKLION ARCHAEOLOGICAL MUSEUM,
CRETE, GREECE

The Boxer Rhyton is decorated in relief
across four registers. The first and third
depict rotational and paired boxing, with
pugilists kitted out in helmets, boots and
gloves. Colonnades suggest a palatial setting,
perhaps even a central court. The fourth
may depict an event combining wrestling
and boxing, similar to the brutal pankration
of later Greek history. The second register
depicted bull-sports; while the lone
surviving acrobat is gored through the lower
back and presumably killed, others were
probably shown leaping successfully. Such
ritualized combats could have served as
martial training for young men approaching
military age and participation may have
been considered a rite of passage.

The Harvester Vase

c. 1675–1460 BCE
Steatite • Height (preserved): 10.1 cm (4 in.) • Late Minoan I • From the royal villa at Aghia Triadha, near Phaistos, Crete

HERAKLION
ARCHAEOLOGICAL
MUSEUM, CRETE, GREECE

Originally covered with gold leaf, the surviving section of the Harvester vase depicts an open-air procession of agricultural labourers. Dressed in loincloths and caps, they carry hoes across their shoulders and bags of seed at their waists and are led by an older man in ritual dress carrying a crook. Singers follow to the rear, including one playing a sistrum (rattle), while a lone dancer weaves through the procession in a comedic performance. The event may be an annual sowing festival comparable to the old English Plough Monday.

The Fisherman Fresco

c. 1675–1600 BCE
Lime plaster • Height: 1.5 m (58 in.) • Late Cycladic I • From the West House at Akrotiri, Thera (Santorini)

NATIONAL ARCHAEOLOGICAL MUSEUM, ATHENS, GREECE

Although shown with several brace of dolphin-fish, this youth is not a simple fisherman. His head is shaved, apart from two tumbling locks to the front and rear, and he is naked, save for a red thread around his neck. These attributes identify the figure as an adorant and suggest that the fish may have been intended for a deity. In the fresco's original position, the fisherman's gaze was directed towards an offering table, decorated with marine motifs, positioned on a windowsill in the northwest corner of the room. In a community whose existence was determined by the sea, it, and a similar figure on the adjacent wall, may have served as a signpost for others wishing to make a similar offering.

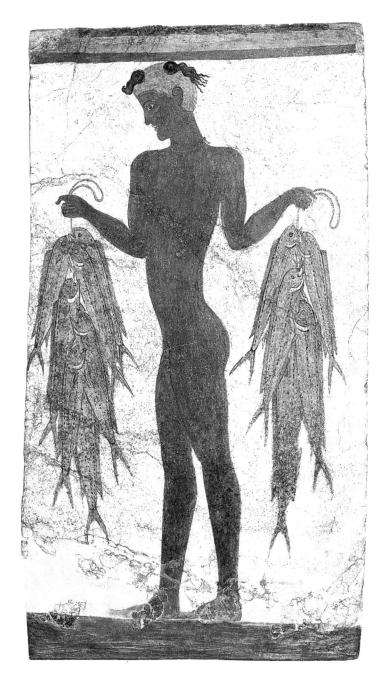

SIGNET RINGS

c. 1675–1410 BCE and *c.* 1460–1410 BCE

*Gold • Width (centre): 5.7 cm (2¼ in.), width (top right): 2.1 cm
(¾ in.) • Late Helladic I–II and Late Minoan II • From Tiryns, Argolid,
Greece (centre) and the Isopata Cemetery, Knossos, Crete (top right)*

NATIONAL ARCHAEOLOGICAL MUSEUM,
ATHENS, GREECE (CENTRE);
HERAKLION ARCHAEOLOGICAL MUSEUM,
CRETE, GREECE (TOP RIGHT)

At almost 6 cm (2¼ in.) in width, the Tiryns signet ring
(centre) is the largest example known. It was already a
centuries-old heirloom when it was gathered together
with other objects of gold, ivory and precious stone,
placed inside a bronze cauldron, covered with
a Cypriot tripod stand and buried in a pit
surrounded by weapons and scrap bronze.
This hoard of metalwork is known today
as the Tiryns Treasure. Once thought to
be a looter's haul, it was probably buried
by a member of a local elite ruling from
Tiryns at the very end of the Bronze
Age, perhaps as an offering or as a
result of social unrest that accompanied
the collapse of palace society on the
mainland. It depicts a procession of
lion-headed Genii (daemons) carrying
libation vessels towards an enthroned
goddess who holds a rhyton aloft and rests
her feet on a footstool. The Isopata ring
(top right) depicts a group of four elaborately
dressed females dancing ecstatically in a natural
setting filled with lilies. A fifth, smaller female
figure is just visible to the rear. This is commonly
interpreted as an epiphany scene, with the smaller
goddess descending from above, although it may actually
depict an initiation ritual for young women. Rings of
this type were certainly elite objects, although particular
imagery may have identified religious rank.

The Snake Goddess and attendant

c. 1460–1410 BCE

Faience • Height of goddess (restored): 29.5 cm (11¾ in.), height of attendant (restored): 34.2 cm (13½ in.) • Late Minoan II • From the Temple Repository at Knossos, Crete

HERAKLION ARCHAEOLOGICAL
MUSEUM, CRETE, GREECE

The faience snake goddess (left) and attendant (right), perhaps also a deity, were found in fragments among a collection of objects at Knossos that appear to represent the paraphernalia of an official religion reserved for the palatial elite. Wearing religious dress and an elaborate hat with a feline perched atop, the goddess has been reconstructed holding aloft a pair of snakes. Snakes also wend their way around the arms, torso and crown of the attendant. The goddess may represent one incarnation of the 'Mistress of Animals' (Potnia) referred to in Linear B. The deity is normally associated with nature and fertility, although the snakes suggest a chthonic component.

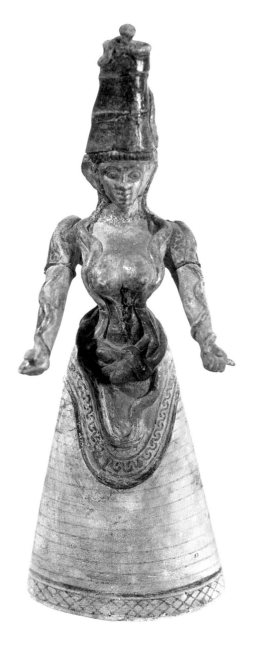

The Ivory Triad

c. 1600–1410 BCE

Ivory • Height: 7.8 cm (3 in.) • Late Helladic II
• From the acropolis of Mycenae, Argolid, Greece

NATIONAL ARCHAEOLOGICAL MUSEUM,
ATHENS, GREECE

Probably made by a Minoan craftsperson, this
intricate ivory group depicts a young robed
girl at the knee of a pair of crouching, possibly
adolescent, women. The eyebrows and eyelashes
of the intact adult were inlaid; perhaps too,
those of her companion. Her partially
shaved head, the Minoan-style flounced
skirts and exposed breasts confer a
religious significance. The group
is often considered divine,
although the focus may have
been on the role of women
as care-givers, or on the
principal life stages of
childhood, puberty
and adulthood.

Bull's head rhyton

c. 1700–1460 BCE

Steatite, jasper and shell • Length (muzzle to top of head): 20 cm (7¾ in.) • Middle Minoan III–Late Minoan I • From the Little Palace at Knossos, Crete

HERAKLION ARCHAEOLOGICAL MUSEUM, CRETE, GREECE

This is the most impressive of a small number of bull rhyta known from the Aegean. The presence of this and other examples at Knossos reflects the prominence of the bull in the political propaganda of the palace. The face and ears are steatite, the eyes are rock crystal, bordered with jasper, and the muzzle is inlaid with tridacna (clam shell) from the Red Sea. The horns have been restored in gilt wood. A small graffito on the back of the neck suggests that they may originally have been sawn, perhaps following a practice observed during bull sacrifice. No bull rhyton has been excavated intact, and it is possible that they were used in lieu of real animals during rituals in which they were deliberately destroyed.

The Aghia Triadha Sarcophagus

c. 1370–1315 BCE

Limestone • Length: 1.4 m (4½ ft), height: 0.9 m (3 ft) • Late Minoan IIIA2 • From Chamber Tomb 4 at Aghia Triadha, near Phaistos, Crete

HERAKLION ARCHAEOLOGICAL MUSEUM, CRETE, GREECE

This sarcophagus offers a unique narrative depiction of funerary ritual that incorporates Minoan and Mycenaean elements, perhaps to convey a political message at a time when Crete may have fallen under Mycenaean control. Side A depicts a daytime scene with females pouring libations beneath a pair of double axes accompanied by a male lyre player, and a night scene showing men moving towards a figure who may represent the deceased. Side B depicts a pair of women sacrificing a bull, accompanied by a male flautist. On the terminal ends are female divinities in Mycenaean chariots drawn by griffin and others drawn by wild goats.

Female head

c. 1315–1190 BCE
Stucco • Height (preserved):
16.8 cm (6½ in.) • Probably
Late Helladic IIIB • From a
building close to the cult centre
at Mycenae, Argolid, Greece

NATIONAL ARCHAEOLOGICAL
MUSEUM, ATHENS, GREECE

The stucco-plaster head known
as 'the sphinx' is a rare example of
Mycenaean plastic art and may represent the
remains of a female cult statue once venerated
within a shrine or sanctuary on the Mycenaean
acropolis. Her low cap is of a type seen on elite
females, female deities and sphinx elsewhere in
Mycenaean art. Four rosettes, perhaps tattoos,
decorate the chin, cheeks and forehead. Nothing
survives of the body, and so it is not clear whether the
head belongs to a couchant sphinx or to a goddess,
perhaps enthroned as shown on the Tiryns ring
(see page 118).

Collapse and Renewal

Expanding networks of trade and communication during the Early Iron Age resulted in the adoption of eastern themes into Greek art. Among the most striking examples of this is the addition of cast bronze griffin protomes to the tripod bowls offered at Greek sanctuaries.

The collapse of the Mycenaean palace system was not as catastrophic as once imagined. A handful of mainland sites show evidence of reconstruction and other, formerly minor, sites began to rise to prominence against the post-palatial backdrop of devolved authority and social and economic instability. An increasingly regionalized post-palatial Mycenaean culture persisted for at least another century, before giving way to the first phase of the Early Iron Age.

The site of Lefkandi on the west coast of Euboea was among the most significant, yet even here periodic destruction and fluctuating fortune suggest that life was not entirely charmed. Warrior burials on the mainland and the islands reflect the association of warfare and power during the period and, on Crete, an increase in inland and upland 'refuge' sites may be explained by a need for greater security in the face of an increase in raiding and piracy. By the later 11th century BCE, connections are visible between Euboea and the Greek mainland, the Cyclades, Crete, Cyprus and the eastern Aegean and Syro-Palestinian coast. During this period, the use of iron became more common, the cumulative effect of increasing familiarity and the difficulties of sourcing copper and tin from the East. Local craftsmen began to produce low numbers of objects in imitation of foreign styles in order to meet a new demand for exotic products. Imported items began to be buried with the dead, as the funeral again became an important arena for social competition, a practice that reached an apogee in the early 10th century BCE with the monumental Heroön at Lefkandi.

An 'ash altar' stood in the Altis (sacred grove) at Olympia perhaps as early as the later 11th century BCE, and there are hints of cult continuity from Bronze to Iron Age at a handful of sites, including Kalapodi in Phocis, Kato Symi on Crete and perhaps Mount Lykaion in Arcadia. During the 10th and 9th centuries BCE, however, there was a steady rise in the number of Greek sanctuaries and the volume and variety of dedications. Cult spaces adopted an increased significance as the principal location for displays of wealth and power. They were, politically, extremely important. Participation in cult helped to reinforce the collective identity of fledgling poleis (city-states), while the location of sanctuaries could aid in the definition of their territory. Identities (and rivalries) found a new mode of expression in the foundation of the Olympiad – the Panhellenic festival of Zeus at Olympia – if not by its traditional foundation date of 776 BCE, then probably by the end of the century. Temples are visible on the mainland and Crete from at least the mid 10th century BCE, although they are usually small and built largely of wood and mud brick. By the end of the 8th century BCE, the first monumental examples are evident at Samos and Eretria.

Although groups moved across the Aegean throughout the earlier stages of the Iron Age, the 8th century BCE traditionally marks the beginning of a colonizing movement that

This terracotta model from the Argive Heraion dates to c. 700 BCE. It may offer some idea of the appearance of the non-monumental temples during the Early Iron Age, although its identification as a cult building is not certain.

expanded Greek influence across the Mediterranean and which fed back into Greek art and material culture. Traditionally, the first major settlement outside of the Aegean was founded by Euboean settlers at Pithekoussai, on the island of Ischia in the Bay of Naples. *c.* 750 BCE. It seems likely that some Euboean colonists really did settle here, although it can be difficult to distinguish colonies (apoikia) from trading posts (emporion), or even simply from less-prescribed socio-cultural interactions. Details of early foundations that do survive are invariably skewed by the lens of Classical politics, when the potential reward of political alliance more than justified the conjuring of some false ancestral link between colony and mother-city.

The Kerameikos derives its name from the fact that it served as a potter's quarter during the Early Iron Age. During this period, it began to be used as a cemetery and subsequently developed into one of the most important burial areas of Athens.

Nevertheless, trade and movement undoubtedly occurred. It is because of the interaction of Greek and Phoenician groups in the east Mediterranean, and the Greek adaptation of the Phoenician alphabet, that literacy returned to Greece, perhaps as early as *c.* 800 BCE. It is this that allowed Homer to fix his definitive version of the *Iliad* and the *Odyssey* and Hesiod his *Theogony* and *Works and Days* (*c.* 700 BCE), alongside others whose work is now lost altogether or partially preserved in that of later authors.

Stirrup jar

c. 1190–1050 BCE

Terracotta • Height: 11.4 cm (4½ in.) • Late Minoan IIIC • From Tourloti, Siteia, Crete

UNIVERSITY OF PENNSYLVANIA
MUSEUM OF ANTHROPOLOGY
AND ARCHAEOLOGY,
PHILADELPHIA,USA

In the aftermath of the collapse of the palace system, Mycenaean pictorial pottery production witnessed a final flourish. With a shift away from the stylistic uniformity of the palatial koine, a range of elaborate regional styles emerged. The so-called Fringed Style, seen here, is one of a number developed on Crete and it takes its name from the extensive use of short strokes around central motifs, in this case a stylized octopus. Vessels such as this reflect a renewed local demand for high-status items.

Centaur

c. 1000–900 BCE

Terracotta • Height: 35.5 cm (14 in.) • Protogeometric
• From the Toumba Cemetery at Lefkandi, Euboea

ARCHAEOLOGICAL MUSEUM OF
ERETRIA, EUBOEA, GREECE

This terracotta is the earliest certain representation
in Greek art of the human-horse hybrid known as
the centaur. Equally significantly, the figure bears
a deep incision just below the left kneecap, which
has been used to identify it as an image of Chairon,
teacher of the hero Achilles, who was held to have
been killed accidentally by Herakles, shot in the leg
by an arrow tipped with the blood of the Lernean
hydra. If correct, this figure
also represents the earliest
evidence for the myth
of Chairon, and by
extension, the first
artistic depiction
of mythic narrative.

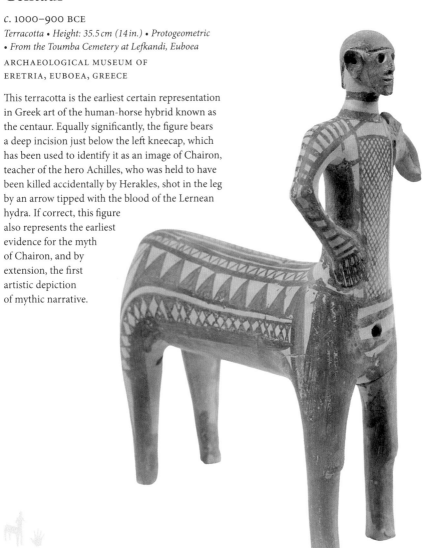

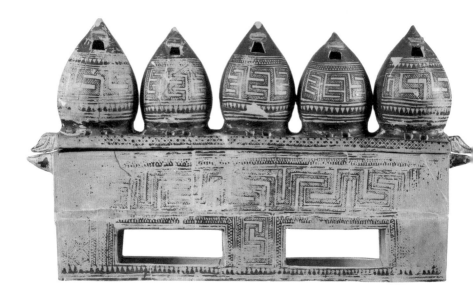

Modelled chest

c. 850 BCE

Terracotta • Height: 25.3 cm (10 in.), Length: 44.5 cm (17½ in.)
• Early Geometric II–Middle Geometric I • From the Tomb of the Rich
Athenian Lady, Areopagus, Athens, Greece

MUSEUM OF THE ANCIENT AGORA, ATHENS, GREECE

Recent analyses have shown that the 'rich Athenian lady' with whom this chest was buried was in the third trimester of pregnancy, and raise the possibility that she died from complications or during labour. This fact may have influenced her burial, perhaps granting her membership of the aoroi (untimely dead). This chest, with its modelled granaries, may reference the agricultural wealth of contemporary Athenian aristocracy, though others have interpreted the domes as beehives and read a chthonic symbolism.

Pendant earrings

c. 850 BCE

*Gold • Length: 6.5 cm (2½ in.) • Early Geometric
II–Middle Geometric I • From the Tomb of the
Rich Athenian Lady, Areopagus, Athens, Greece*

MUSEUM OF THE ANCIENT AGORA,
ATHENS, GREECE

In addition to the modelled chest (see
opposite), the 'rich Athenian lady' was
accompanied by a further eighty grave
offerings. This group comprised pottery
and terracotta objects, as well as jewelry
and personal items, including an elaborate
necklace incorporating approximately 1,100
faience beads and others of rock crystal and
glass. The use of filigree and granulation
implies that the craftsman responsible
for these earrings was familiar with Near
Eastern techniques; it is less likely that they
were imported. Pendant from each are a set
of three pomegranates, a fruit with a symbolic
association to death and the afterlife during
the Archaic and Classical period.

Pyxis with modelled quadriga

c. 750–735 BCE
Terracotta • Height: 24 cm (9½ in.), diameter: 35 cm (13¾ in.)
• Late Geometric IB • From the Kerameikos, Athens, Greece

NATIONAL ARCHAEOLOGICAL MUSEUM, ATHENS, GREECE

As in earlier periods, pyxides of the Middle to Late Geometric period were used to store jewelry or cosmetics. In addition to their intricate decoration, these vessels are sometimes augmented with up to four modelled horses, serving as a handle for the lid. The four-horse chariot appears in the *Iliad* and such depictions are often linked with the horse-owning aristocratic class of Archaic Athenian society, known as the hippeis. However, they appear most often as offerings in female graves, and those found with males seem to have had their horses broken off, suggesting that social and religious symbolism informed their funerary use.

The Dipylon Oinochoe

c. 750–725 BCE
Ceramic • Height: 22 cm (8¾ in.) • Late
Geometric IB–II • From the Dipylon
Cemetery, Kerameikos, Athens, Greece

NATIONAL ARCHAEOLOGICAL
MUSEUM, ATHENS, GREECE

This oinochoe (wine jug) bears an Ionian
Greek poetic inscription identifying it
as a prize in a dancing competition: 'the
dancer who dances most delicately [will
have me as a prize]'. The occasion may
have been a symposion (drinking party)
and the inscription hurriedly scratched
by the host or one of his guests. This vessel
provides evidence for the return of literacy
to Greece following the adaptation of the
Phoenician alphabet. This innovation
may have taken place in the eastern
Mediterranean, where Greek and
Phoenician traders came into contact,
and is arguably the single most important
development of the Early Iron Age.

THE CUP OF NESTOR

c. 730 BCE

Ceramic • Height: 10.3 cm (4 in.) • Late Geometric II • From Cremation Grave 168
at Pithekoussai, Ischia, Italy

VILLA ARBUSTO MUSEUM, LACCO AMENO, ITALY

Manufactured on Rhodes, this skyphos (drinking cup) was found in the grave of a young boy in the Greek colony of Pithekoussai and preserves a hexameter drinking song in Euboean Greek: '[...] Nestor's cup I am, good to drink from, whoever drinks this cup empty, will soon be seized by desire for fair-crowned Aphrodite.' In the light-hearted comparison with the golden cup of the mythical King of Pylos, this skyphos provides the earliest independent reference to Homer's *Iliad,* or to the stories on which it was based.

One of the most influential literary works in the history of Western civilization, the *Iliad* is a war epic and details the final phase

To the ancient Greeks, Homer was their first and greatest poet, and was considered by Plato to be the 'best and most divine'. Beyond his poetry, however, almost nothing is known about Homer the man, or his life.

of a ten-year conflict fought between Greece and Troy. It incorporates a number of oral traditions, some certainly prehistoric in origin, which would have been memorized and performed to music. There may have been multiple versions in circulation; however, the development of the alphabet allowed Homer, perhaps writing on the west coast of Asia Minor, to fix a definitive version of the epic, with which he would become synonymous. Aristocratic males such as those who used the Cup of Nestor became avid consumers of Homer's work. Its themes, and the 'heroic' Greek past, would, in turn, pervade all aspects of ideal Greek culture.

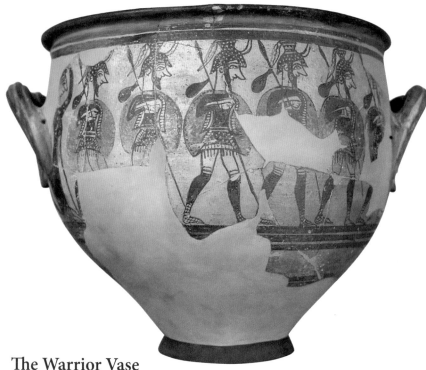

The Warrior Vase

c. 1190–1050 BCE
Ceramic • Height: 43 cm (17 in.),
diameter: 48–50.5 cm (19–20 in.) • Late Helladic IIIC
• From the House of the Warrior Krater, Mycenae, Argolid, Greece

NATIONAL ARCHAEOLOGICAL MUSEUM, ATHENS, GREECE

This pictorial krater is decorated with two units of spearmen
and a partially preserved female who raises her hand in a
probable gesture of lament. The vessel was probably a grave
offering; it may even have served as a grave marker, and its
themes may be funerary. However, the increase in scenes
of combat and warfare during this period may also reflect a
post-palatial landscape in which clashes between emerging
local rulers, as well as raiding and banditry, were common.

Warrior figurine

c. 700 BCE

Bronze • Height: 27.6 cm
(10¾ in.) • Late Geometric II
• From Karditsa, Thessaly, Greece

NATIONAL ARCHAEOLOGICAL MUSEUM,
ATHENS, GREECE

This warrior, like the Argive cuirass (see
page 141), belongs to a period before the
development of hoplite warfare. Armed
with a single spear, now lost, this figure has
no armour beyond a belt or girdle, perhaps
akin to the *zoster* belt of Menelaos described
in Homer's *Iliad*. He wears a high helmet
capable of supporting a crest, and carries an
oval Dipylon shield with deep hemispherical
cut-outs. The type is known on Geometric
pottery, although it is unclear whether it
was a purely artistic invention. It has been
suggested that the figure represents Achilles.

The Argos Panoply

c. 720 BCE

Bronze and iron • Height: 50 cm (19¾ in.)
and 46 cm (18 in.) • Late Geometric II
• From Grave 45, Argos, Greece

ARCHAEOLOGICAL MUSEUM OF
ARGOS, GREECE

At the end of the Geometric period, bronze
armour was re-introduced to the mainland,
after an apparent absence of *c.* 400 years.
This bell cuirass or thorax consisted of
individual breast and back plates that flared
outwards at the base to deflect downward
blows and, perhaps, aid horsemanship.
It is the earliest example yet known and
belonged to an individual who may have
been a local leader. The crested kegelhelm-
type helmet may have been aesthetically
impressive, though uneven weighting and a
lack of protection for the face made the type
relatively impractical.

Belly-handled amphora

c. 760–750 BCE

Ceramic • Height: 1.6 m (5¼ ft) • Late
Geometric IA • From the Dipylon Cemetery,
Kerameikos, Athens, Greece

NATIONAL ARCHAEOLOGICAL
MUSEUM, ATHENS, GREECE

Manufactured in Athens towards the
end of the Early Iron Age, monumental
Dipylon amphorae were set up above
the graves of elite women as markers
and memorials, and had a hole in the
base through which libations might
be offered to the dead. This example
is attributed to the so-called Dipylon
Master, an Athenian artist often
recognized as the first of the
great Greek vase painters
and credited with a variety
of innovations in ceramic art.
Accompanied by geometric
designs across the body and
friezes of deer and goats on
the neck, the principal scene
on this vessel depicts prothesis
or the laying out of the
deceased in advance of burial.

Kalathos

c. 1190–1050 BCE

Ceramic • Height: 14.9 cm (5¾ in.), diameter: 15.4 cm (6 in.) • Late Helladic IIIC • From Tomb 12 at Ialysos, Rhodes

BRITISH MUSEUM, LONDON, UK

The flaring bowl known as a kalathos probably takes its inspiration from woven basketry. Examples with modelled figures at the rim are known in this period at Ialysos and at Perati in Attica and, along with other pottery types, attest to continued maritime trade links between the eastern Aegean and the mainland following the collapse of the palace system. The vessel itself was used for funerary rituals and the figures here represent mourning women in gestures of lament; two beat their arms to the chest, while the third clasps her hands at the neck, tearing at her hair. A fourth figure has been lost.

Horse figurine

c. 800–700 BCE

Bronze • Height: 17.6 cm (7 in.) • Middle–Late Geometric
• Provenance unknown

METROPOLITAN MUSEUM OF ART,
NEW YORK CITY, USA

During the Early Iron Age, regional sanctuaries
assumed importance as meeting places where local
leaders might display their power and piety through
the conspicuous dedication of high-value objects.
Horse ownership was itself a sign of status and, with
both martial connotations and symbolic associations
to Athena and Poseidon, horses dominated the highly
stylized regional figural traditions of the period.
Substantial numbers in both terracotta and bronze were
offered as votives in the major sanctuaries of southern
Greece. It is possible that some were manufactured and
sold within the sanctuaries themselves.

TRIPOD CAULDRON

c. 900–800 BCE

Bronze • Height (including handles): 65 cm (25½ in.) • Early Geometric
• From the Sanctuary of Zeus at Olympia

ARCHAEOLOGICAL MUSEUM OF OLYMPIA, GREECE

This tripod cauldron is a Bronze Age shape that formed a major category of votive offering during the Early Iron Age. They were, first and foremost, cooking vessels, although in the *Iliad* tripod vessels were awarded as prizes at the funeral games of Patroclus, and surviving inscriptions make clear their function as prizes in other types of elite competition.

This example is the earliest to have survived at Olympia. Its modest size and solid construction reflect the function for which it was originally intended. Over time, however, and with an increasing focus on display, these vessels became much larger, less robust and more decorative, including scenes of myth or elaborate cast attachments. By the end of the Early Iron Age, those still small enough to be functional may have been used for mixing wine, perhaps during events in the sanctuary itself. Monumental examples, however, were designed primarily to convey information about the status of their owners, their ability to access metal and skilled metalsmiths, and their privileged relationship with the god or goddess to whom they were offered, in an environment of competitive dedication among elites.

In its earliest phases, the sanctuary at Olympia likely served distinctly local needs as a meeting place where leaders might display their own power. As competition between these individuals and their followers increased, so too did the need to undertake public display on an even grander scale.

Pedestalled krater

c. 750–735 BCE
Ceramic • Height: 1.1 m (3½ ft) • Late Geometric IB
• Provenance unknown (said to be from Attica)
METROPOLITAN MUSEUM OF ART,
NEW YORK CITY, USA

As monumental amphorae seem to have marked the
graves of elite Athenian women, monumental kraters
appear to have been commissioned for those of elite
Athenian men. This example is the latest in a series
produced in the workshop of an artist known today
as the Hirschfeld Painter. It depicts the prothesis of
the dead man on a raised bier, his shroud lifted away,
flanked by his family and other mourners who tear
at their hair in grief. A procession of charioteers and
infantry appears below, perhaps a depiction of the
games that accompanied elite Early Iron Age funerals.

City-State
and Citizen

This bearded hoplite from the area of the sanctuary of Athena Chalkioikos at Sparta is sometimes identified as Leonidas, the Spartan king who fell at Thermopylae. Others identify him as the general Pausanias who led the victory at Plataea, and others still, a participant in the hoplitodromos or foot race in armour.

The Archaic to Classical period is characterized by the emergence of the polis (city-state), although alternative political systems persisted in some regions long after its appearance. These cities developed through the agglomeration of smaller Early Iron Age settlements, usually around a defensible hill or acropolis, although foundation traditions are plagued by self-conscious historical myth-making and later political rhetoric.

The process was accompanied by legal and constitutional reform that served to create (or maintain) a sense of community identity and provided social and political stability to early centres. The earliest surviving law in stone, from Dreros in eastern Crete, dates to *c.* 650 BCE. It, and other early laws, already evidence democratic concerns and the role of the citizen body in the oversight of elite offices and in political decision-making. Nevertheless, many city-states experienced tyranny. The term denoted only that rule was unconstitutional. Its Archaic meaning was far less pejorative than the modern sense, and while later sources can be critical of tyranny, some tyrants sponsored festivals

The Ionic Erechtheion was one of several structures erected on the Acropolis under the Periklean programme that saw construction of the Parthenon. Its most striking feature is its south porch, where six caryatids take the place of supporting columns, sculpted contrapposto to make their task seem effortless.

and public building programmes to court popular support, and some cities thrived.

The construction of monumental public buildings and the formalization of urban space accompanied political developments in many cities. Both local and Panhellenic sanctuaries also saw considerable investment. The earliest monumental stone temple at Olympia, dedicated to Hera, appeared in *c.* 600 BCE, and at Delphi the early 6th century BCE witnessed a huge amount of building. The development of sanctuary architecture also paralleled the foundation of new Panhellenic festivals at Delphi, Nemea and Isthmia that, along with the Olympiad, made up the periodos (institutionalized festival circuit). The Greater Panathenaia at Athens, the most important festival outside of the circuit, is traditionally thought to have been founded in 566 BCE.

Conflict between Archaic city-states led to advances in the tactics of land and naval warfare that would come to typify the wars of the Classical period. Changes in weapons and armour accompanied the emergence of the hoplite as a new heavy-troop type eventually characterized by a tightly ranked fighting formation known as the phalanx. Its development is likely to have been a gradual process, although something

resembling its Classical form is visible in art from the 7th century BCE. Hoplites were not professional soldiers, but citizen farmers who fought around the agricultural calendar and owned land in the chora (hinterland). Compared with the city, the Archaic-Classical chora is less well understood, although it is possible to recognize a landscape filled with farmsteads, dispersed villages, rural shrines, cemeteries and border-forts linked by a network of roads and routeways.

During the 6th century BCE, the first Greek coins were minted, replacing the earlier use of iron spits and other metal objects in economic transaction. The emergence of the black-figure technique of pottery painting at Corinth (from *c.* 720 BCE) and its later refinement at Athens (from *c.* 630 BCE) permitted a shift towards narrative art on pottery, and even greater detail was made possible with the red-figure technique (from *c.* 530 BCE). The development of new shapes paralleled the formalization of the domestic symposion (drinking party). The works of Archilochus of Paros, Sappho of Lesbos, Alcman and Tyrtaeus of Sparta heralded a new wave of poetic output. The victory of Thespis in the first tragic contest at Athens in 534 BCE prepared the ground for the great tragedians of the 5th century BCE (Aeschylus, Sophocles and Euripides) and for the development of comedy. Life-sized statuary appeared in the mid-7th century BCE, and a shift towards realism was apparent during the early 5th century. Sculpture appeared on the monumental temples and buildings of the new Doric and Ionic architectural orders. Classical wall paintings, almost without exception, do not survive, although later descriptions give an idea of their form and the high esteem in which they were held.

Politically, the later 5th century BCE was dominated by the Peloponnesian War between Athens and Sparta and their respective allies (431–403 BCE). The Spartan triumph that marked the end of this conflict, achieved with Persian support, was, however, relatively short-lived. The early 4th century BCE was a period of political instability and it was this instability that facilitated the rise of a new rival power in the north: Macedon.

The Myrina Hoard

c. 550–450 BCE

*Silver • Height (olpe): 11.5 cm (4½ in.) • Archaic • From Myrina,
Thessaly, Greece*

NUMISMATIC MUSEUM, ATHENS, GREECE

A coin hoard excavated beneath the Temple of Artemis at Ephesus
places the development of coinage in electrum (an alloy of gold and
silver) in Lydia (western Turkey) in *c.* 650 BCE. The first silver issues
appeared in the East roughly a century later, and the earliest Greek
issues appeared on Aegina soon afterwards. The island very quickly
developed as a centre of coin production, with huge numbers of
'turtles' (named for the design on their obverse) minted during the
later 6th century BCE. This hoard of 149 Aeginetan staters, buried
in an olpe (wine jug), includes both the earlier turtles and a later type
depicting a common tortoise, sometimes associated with Aegina's loss
of independence to Athens.

Aryballoi

c. 625–550 BCE

Ceramic • Height of octopus aryballos: 6.7 cm (2¾ in.), Nearchos aryballos: 7.8 cm (3 in.), Odysseus and the Sirens aryballos: 10.2 cm (4 in.) • Archaic • Provenance unknown

PRINCETON UNIVERSITY ART MUSEUM, USA; METROPOLITAN MUSEUM OF ART, NEW YORK CITY, USA; MUSEUM OF FINE ARTS, BOSTON, USA

With a broad rim and a narrow mouth, these aryballoi (oil flasks) were designed to hold perfumed oil. Developed at Corinth, and subsequently produced in their thousands, they differ in quality, although some are exquisitely realized. Decorative motifs vary considerably, as here, drawing on themes from society, nature and myth. The Nearchos aryballos is exceptional for the miniature battle between pygmies and cranes that adorns its rim, incorporating some sixteen figures in a space only 1 cm (½ in.) high and some 13 cm (5 in.) in length. Satyrs, tritons and depictions of Hermes and Perseus decorate the handle, which Nearchos, the potter and painter, has signed.

Athenian tetradrachm

c. 450–406 BCE
Silver • Diameter: 2.5 cm (1 in.), weight: 17.2 g
(½ oz) • Classical • Provenance unknown

BRITISH MUSEUM, LONDON, UK

The appearance of the Athenian tetradrachm (commonly
known as glaukes or 'owls') coincides broadly with
the end of the Peisistratid tyranny (*c.* 514 BCE) and the
development of Athenian democracy. Minted in silver
from the mines at Thorikos to the south of the city, this
four-drachma coin was equivalent to four days' wages for
a skilled labourer. It is decorated on the obverse with the
helmeted head of Athena and on the reverse with the owl,
the olive (signifying peace and prosperity) and a waning
moon. Athena represents the city of Athens, while the
owl represents the wisdom of Athena (as the city). The
easily recognizable three-letter inscription 'AΘE' is an
abbreviation of AΘHNAION, meaning 'of the Athenians'.

Votive plaque

c. 575–550 BCE

Terracotta • Height: 7.2 cm (2¾ in.), length: 10 cm (4 in.) • Archaic
• From Penteskouphia, near Corinth, Greece

LOUVRE, PARIS, FRANCE

The Corinthian site of Penteskouphia has yielded more than 1,000 pinakes (votive plaques). Pierced and probably suspended from a tree at, or close to, a rural sanctuary to Poseidon, inscriptions commonly name the deities to whom they were offered. Some sixty plaques depict craftsmen at work. Overside, this example depicts the extraction of clay from a pit by one Onymon, while here a potter (or assistant), Sordis, manipulates the kiln vent. Such scenes may reflect a desire for divine support during the firing process.

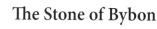

The Stone of Bybon

c. 625–575 BCE

Sandstone • Height: 33 cm (13 in.), length: 68 cm (26¾ in.)
• Archaic • From southeast of the Pelopion at Olympia, Greece

ARCHAEOLOGICAL MUSEUM OF OLYMPIA, GREECE

With a carved handgrip on the underside, this block
preserves an inscription written in the boustrophedon
format (left-right and then right-left on alternate lines)
that declares: 'Bybon son of Phola, has lifted me over [his]
head with one hand.' Weightlifting was a training exercise
for athletes, rather than an official event at the Olympiad.
Nevertheless, Bybon's feat must have been considered
so extraordinary as to warrant dedication of the stone at
the sanctuary. It weighs approximately 143.5 kg (316 lb). A
similar feat of strength is referenced on a contemporary, if
much larger stone (approximately 480 kg/1058 lb), found
near Sellada on Thera, which states: 'Eumastas, son of
Kritobolos, lifted me from the ground.'

The Akmatidas Halter

c. 550 BCE

Stone • Height: 9.2 cm (3¾ in.), length: 25.5 cm (10 in.) • Archaic
• From the Sanctuary of Zeus at Olympia, Greece

ARCHAEOLOGICAL MUSEUM OF OLYMPIA, GREECE

The exact character of the Archaic and Classical long jump remains a
matter of debate, although the use of handheld weights of approximately
1.5–2.5 kg (3¼–5½ lb) suggests a standing start, with final distances probably
reflecting the aggregate total of multiple jumps. The event did not constitute
an individual competition but rather formed part of the pentathlon. The
inscription on this halter identifies it as a dedication by a Spartan Olympic
victor who won akoniti ('without dust', or by default): 'Akmatidas of
Lakedaimonia having won the five without dust dedicated [this].'

Boundary stone

c. 500 BCE
Marble • Height: 1.2 m (4 ft),
originally exposed: 0.7 m (2¼ ft)
• Archaic • Found in situ *west of the Middle*
Stoa, Agora, Athens, Greece

MUSEUM OF THE ANCIENT AGORA,
ATHENS, GREECE

Although rather unassuming, this horos
(boundary stone) is representative
of important changes in the urban,
social and political structure of Athens
attributed to the statesman Kleisthenes
at the transition from the 6th to the 5th
century BCE. As the Agora developed
into the centre of the new democracy,
its limits were formally prescribed. This
horos was one of a series set up where
streets entered the space and bears
the retrograde inscription: 'I am the
boundary of the Agora'. Supported by
religious sanction, they prevented the
encroachment of private buildings into
this public space and restricted access
to criminals and other groups.

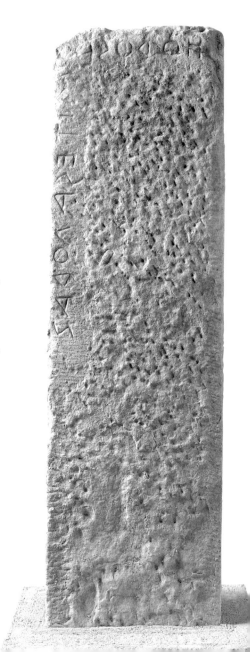

Panathenaic amphora

c. 530 BCE

Ceramic • Height: 62.2 cm (24½ in.)
• Archaic • Provenance unknown

METROPOLITAN MUSEUM OF ART,
NEW YORK CITY, USA

Like the Olympiad, the festival of the
Greater Panathenaia (traditionally
founded in *c.* 566 BCE) was held every
four years and incorporated a variety of
athletic events. The prize for victory was
Attic olive oil. Each Panathenaic amphora
would have held roughly one metretes
(approximately 37 litres/9¾ gal) and the
winner of the footrace for which this
vessel was awarded could have received
as many as seventy in total. The event
itself is depicted on the reverse, while
the goddess Athena, to whom the
festival was dedicated, appears on
the obverse, with the inscription
'tôn athenethen athlôn' (one
of the prizes from Athens).

Black-figure amphora

c. 500–490 BCE

Ceramic • Height: 36.1 cm (14¼ in.) • Archaic-Classical • Provenance unknown

MUSEUM OF FINE ARTS, BOSTON, USA

Attic black-figure pottery commonly depicted scenes inspired by myth or epic, or the social, political or cultural institutions of Athens. Betraying the contemporary concerns of Athenian citizenry and often transmitting implicit social or political messages, such scenes were eminently more marketable. Scenes that illustrate industry, commerce and the more routine aspects of daily life were much less common. This late example provides a window on to two such activities and may have been a special commission. The obverse depicts a cobbler in his well-equipped workshop tailoring shoes for a female client, while the reverse depicts a pair of smiths in the forge working an object on the anvil.

Female athlete

c. 550–540 BCE
*Bronze • Height: 11.7 cm
(4½ in.) • Archaic • From the
Sanctuary of Zeus at Dodona, Epirus, Greece*

NATIONAL ARCHAEOLOGICAL MUSEUM, ATHENS, GREECE

Women were not permitted to compete in the Olympiad, or
to attend it. Unmarried women were, however, permitted to
compete in a footrace held in the Olympic stadium as part of
a separate quadrennial festival in honour of the goddess Hera.
Originally attached to the shoulder of a bowl or krater, this figure
may depict a Spartan competitor. Sparta appears to have been
alone among poleis in encouraging athletic training among
women, purportedly with the aim of providing the polis with
strong sons. Later sources suggest that their programme included
many of the events that Sparta used to hone these sons for war.

Figurine of a barber

c. 500–480 BCE

Terracotta • Height: 11.6 cm (4½ in.) • Archaic-Classical
• Provenance unknown (said to be from Tanagra, Boeotia, Greece)

MUSEUM OF FINE ARTS, BOSTON, USA

This handmade figurine is one of a larger Boeotian group
that model a variety of everyday activities, including food
preparation, baking, cooking and carpentry. Women appear
more commonly than men, and figures are always
represented in action, either in discussion
with others, or engaged in their task,
providing insight into subject matter
that rarely finds its way into art. This
is particularly true of the barber,
who seems not to have been
represented at all in contemporary
pottery, despite the importance of
grooming, and the barber shop
as a male social space
in Classical society.

Ostraka

c. 487/6 BCE

*Ceramic • Dimensions: various • Classical
• From the Agora, Athens, Greece*

MUSEUM OF THE ANCIENT AGORA,
ATHENS, GREECE

An ostracism was a popular vote designed to protect Athenian democracy through the exile of men with too much power or tyrannical aspirations. A minimum of 6,000 citizen participants were required for a valid vote. Votes were cast using ostraka – potsherds incised or painted with the name of a preferred victim, occasionally accompanied by a derogatory graffito. Exile lasted for a decade, although the ostracized retained their citizen rights. The first Athenian certainly removed in this way was Hipparchus (488/7 BCE), the last may have been Hyperbolus (*c.* 416 BCE). It began as the ultimate democratic check, although its value was later undermined by fraudulent voting designed to remove political rivals.

Basic with wrestlers at the rim

c. 490 BCE

Bronze • Height: 28 cm (11 in.), diameter: 72 cm (28¼ in.)
*• Archaic-Classical • Provenance unknown (said to be from
the region of Picenum, Italy)*

MUSEUM OF FINE ARTS, BOSTON, USA

Wrestling, boxing and the mixed pankration were
thought to serve as martial training for young men
of fighting age. With little evidence from city-states
other than Sparta of institutionalized military training,
young soldiers may have turned to these events to hone
strength. Training took place in an open-air facility
known as the palaestra (from the Greek word 'pale',
meaning 'wrestle'). This basin, perhaps a Laconian
export, depicts upright wrestling in which three throws
were required for a win. The alternative 'on the ground'
style was won by submission. While biting and low-
blows were illegal, finger-breaking was permitted.

Great Code of Gortyn

c. 450 BCE or earlier

*Marble • Height: 50 cm (19¾ in.),
length: 60 cm (23½ in.) • Classical
• From the Roman Odeion,
Gortyn, Crete*

LOUVRE, PARIS, FRANCE

The inscription date of the Great Code of Gortyn is a matter of debate, although many of its laws likely have their origin in the Archaic period, a phase that saw major constitutional reform across Crete and Greece. The boustrophedon text, totalling almost 10 m (33 ft) wide and 2.3 m (7½ ft) high, codifies more than one hundred laws on subjects as diverse as litigation, adoption, religious propriety and, as in this fragment, the rules of inheritance. Punishment included death (perjury) and burning (arson), although rape was punished only by a fine (determined by the status of the rapist and the victim), and there was variation in the protections afforded to different social classes.

Kleroterion

c. 350 BCE

*Marble • Height (preserved): 59 cm (23¼ in.), width: 74 cm
(29¼ in.) • Classical • From the Agora, Athens, Greece*

MUSEUM OF THE ANCIENT AGORA, ATHENS, GREECE

The Athenian court system played a key role in the
democratic process and the kleroterion (allotment device)
was designed to prevent corruption within it. Potential jurors,
selected annually from the citizen body, were issued with a
bronze ticket by which they could be identified. On the day
of trial, these tickets were inserted into the kleroterion. Rows
of jurors were accepted to serve or dismissed by a magistrate
whose decision was based on the release of a white or black
ball, which could be issued from a preloaded bronze tube
within the machine when cranked. The random nature
of this process made bribery almost impossible.

Discus

c. 600–500 BCE

Bronze • Diameter: 16.5 cm (6½ in.), weight: 1.2 kg (2¾ lb)
• Archaic • Provenance unknown (said to be from Kephallonia)

BRITISH MUSEUM, LONDON, UK

A variety of local events populated the Archaic athletic
calender alongside the Panhellenic games at Olympia,
Isthmia, Delphi and Nemea. This discus probably derives
from a local competition held on the Ionian island
of Kephallonia. Subsequently offered as a votive by a
victorious pentathlete, it bears a retrograde inscription to
the Dioskouroi, Kastor and Polydeukes: 'Exoidas dedicated
me to the sons of mighty Zeus, [the] bronze with which he
overcame the great-hearted Kephallenians'.
The inscription directly references
the *Iliad*, perhaps in an attempt
by Exoidas to enhance
his achievement.

Copy of Myron's Discobolos

c. 100–200 CE after original
c. 460–450 BCE

*Marble (after bronze) • Height: 1.5 m
(5 ft) • Roman after Classical original
• From Villa Palombara, Esquiline Hill,
Rome, Italy*

NATIONAL ROMAN MUSEUM,
ROME, ITALY

The Discobolos (Discus Thrower) by
the Athenian Myron immortalizes
the athlete in a moment of absolute
potential at the apex of his draw.
During the Classical period, sculptors
began to experiment with the
relationship between body, time
and space, and Myron is recognized
as the first to master harmony of
movement. Like all of Myron's
works, the original is lost,
although ancient accounts
allow the identification of
later copies. This example
is thought to be the most
accurate, despite the
addition of a trunk at
the leg to support the
weight of the marble.

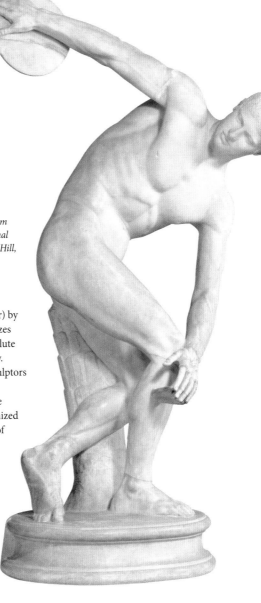

Bilingual amphora

c. 525–520 BCE

Ceramic • Height: 55.5 cm (21¾ in.) • Archaic
• Provenance unknown

MUSEUM OF FINE ARTS, BOSTON, USA

Developed in Athens during the late Archaic period
(*c.* 530 BCE), the red-figure technique of pottery
painting allowed far greater detail and more natural
representation than had previously been possible. As
the popularity of black-figure pottery declined, and
that of red-figure increased, a new type of 'bilingual'
vase appeared that repeated the same scene on
opposite faces in both techniques. Bilingualism very
likely reflected a degree of uncertainty about the new
style among vase painters. Each side of this vessel is
attributed to a different artist, one to the Andokides
Painter and the other to the Lysippides Painter,
although both depict the Homeric heroes Ajax
and Achilles playing a board game.

RED-FIGURE KYLIX

c. 490–480 BCE

Ceramic • Height: 12.8 cm (5 in.), diameter: 33.2 cm (13 in.) • Archaic-Classical
• Provenance unknown

MUSEUM OF FINE ARTS, BOSTON, USA

In the Archaic and Classical Greek house, the andron (men's room) was the location of the most popular past-time of the elite male citizenry: the symposion (drinking party). Symposiasts would recline on kline (couches) positioned left to right around the edge of the room. Each could hold up to two men, and the andron itself would have been of a standard size based on the number of kline it could accommodate (seven, eleven or fifteen). Men would engage in conversation, song or games of skill, as immortalized in Plato's *Symposium*. Women were admitted only as musicians, dancers or courtesans. Painted scenes on drinking vessels regularly depict sex between girls

Signed by the painter Euphronios, this late 6th-century BCE red-figure psykter (wine cooler) depicts a symposion of naked courtesans.

and symposiasts, although it is not clear how far these reflect reality. Proceedings were directed by a symposiarch selected from those in attendance, who would assume responsibility for mixing the wine with water. The symposion employed a repertoire of vessels, each of which had a specific function and many of which would be decorated with scenes of the event itself. The interior tondo of this kylix (drinking cup; opposite) attributed to the painter Makron depicts a reclining symposiast, gesturing in protest towards a woman who has stepped up and grabbed him by the beard. The exterior depicts various groupings of males and females, some clearly anxious suitors.

Red-figure kylix

c. 480 BCE

Ceramic • Height: 12.7 cm (5 in.),
diameter: 27.2 cm (10¾ in.)
• Classical • Provenance unknown

KIMBELL ART MUSEUM,
FORT WORTH, USA

The exterior of this kylix (drinking cup) attributed to the Douris Painter depicts the death of the mythical Theban king Pentheus, torn apart by a group of women, including his mother and aunts, driven into a frenzy by Dionysus, against whom Pentheus had transgressed by denying his divinity. Dionysian imagery is common on sympotic vessels and while the rather gory imagery of Pentheus's final moments would have delighted, the implicit meaning would have carried added weight, for Pentheus was a victim of his own hubris, a concept regarded with deep concern as a threat to public order and new democratic freedoms.

The Athenian Law Against Tyranny

337/6 BCE
Marble • Height: 1.6 m (5¼ ft) • Classical
• From the Agora, Athens, Greece
MUSEUM OF THE ANCIENT AGORA,
ATHENS, GREECE

Macedonian victory over a coalition
of city-states that included Athens,
Thebes and Corinth in 338 BCE
heralded the submission of Greece
(with the exception of Sparta) beneath
Macedonian hegemony. Concerned
for the survival of democracy, the
following year saw the Athenians pass
a law to discourage anti-democratic
or pro-Macedonian action; promising
exemption from prosecution for
citizens who killed anti-democratic
actors and preventing councillors
from functioning in the absence of
the people. This is one of two copies
of the law set up, respectively, at the
entrance to the council house and the
meeting place of the citizen assembly.
The relief depicts the personification
of democracy, Demokratia, crowning
a seated Demos (the people).

Fibula of Attic-Boeotian type

c. 700–675 BCE

Bronze • Length: 20 cm (7¾ in.) • Archaic • From the Idean Cave, Crete

NATIONAL ARCHAEOLOGICAL MUSEUM, ATHENS, GREECE

The large bow fibula (brooch) developed during the Early Iron Age, first in Attica and subsequently in Boeotia, where it became larger and more ornate. This example derives from one of the most important cave sanctuaries of Early Iron Age Crete and represents a rare example of the movement of metalwork from central Greece on to the island. The upperside of the catchplate depicts Herakles in combat with the twin sons of Aktor and Molione, Cteatus and Eurytus (referred to in the *Iliad* and commonly thought to be conjoined), while the reverse depicts a pair of archers poised over a ship.

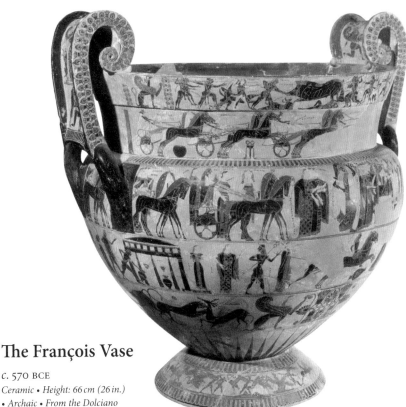

The François Vase

c. 570 BCE

Ceramic • Height: 66 cm (26 in.)
• Archaic • From the Dolciano
grandducal estate, Chiusi, Italy

NATIONAL ARCHAEOLOGICAL
MUSEUM OF FLORENCE, ITALY

The François Vase is significant both as the earliest example of an Attic
volute krater and as a masterpiece of Archaic black-figure pottery
painting. It is signed by both the potter Ergotimos and the painter
Kleitias, and is decorated with scenes of myth, which include 270 figures
and 121 inscriptions, and have at their core the wedding of the parents
of Achilles: Peleus and the sea-nymph Thetis. The intended meaning
behind the decoration is a matter of debate. This item was exceptional,
although it is not clear whether it was exported as a symposion vessel
or whether it served as a prestige object in some other manner.

The Bluebeard Pediment

c. 560–540 BCE

Marble • Height: 0.8 m (2½ ft), width: 3.3 m (10¾ ft) • Archaic
• From the Acropolis, Athens, Greece

ACROPOLIS MUSEUM, ATHENS, GREECE

Although there is some evidence for a 7th-century BCE temple on
the Acropolis, the controversial 'Temple H' is the first stone temple
for which there are meaningful remains. Its construction may have
coincided with the reorganization of the Greater Panathenaia and
reflects the growing importance of monumental temple architecture
to polis identity. The Bluebeard Pediment depicts three male torsos
joined at the waist to a serpentine body, each of which carries a
representation of one of the fundamental elements. The creature's
identity is not clear, although it is commonly associated with the
monstrous Typhon, or Geryon, the subject of Herakles' tenth labour.

The Gigantomachy Pediment

c. 525–500 BCE

Marble • Height: 2 m (6½ ft) • Archaic
• From the Acropolis, Athens, Greece

ACROPOLIS MUSEUM, ATHENS, GREECE

The Archaios Naos (Old Temple) replaced the
earlier 'Temple H'. Numerous fragments of the
building survive, including many reused within
the north wall of the Acropolis. The east
pediment bore a Gigantomachy,
a battle between gods and
giants, rendered in the round.
The goddess Athena (right)
was depicted in the aegis (a
snake-fringed goatskin cloak)
moving across one fallen
giant to strike another with
her spear, now lost. The
temple was a testament
to the new democracy
and the scene may
have reflected the city's
victories over then-
recent challenges to it.

Kritios Boy

c. 490–480 BCE

Marble • Height (preserved): 1.2 m (4 ft) • Classical
• From the Acropolis, Athens, Greece

ACROPOLIS MUSEUM, ATHENS, GREECE

Between the Archaic and Classical periods,
freestanding sculpture experienced an
important shift towards the realistic depiction
of human anatomy and musculature.
Kritios Boy, initially excavated minus his
head (arguably removed by a Persian axe),
is the earliest surviving sculpture in which
this development is evident. The figure
is renowned for its use of contrapposto
(counterpoise), a stance in which the
weight is shifted on to one leg in a more
realistic, asymmetrical way. This would
become a common feature of male statuary
during the Classical period, allowing the
sculptor to explore rhythmos (movement
through the body) and ethos (character),
and demonstrating a serenity of mind that
contributed to the Classical male ideal.

The Polyphemus Amphora

c. 675–650 BCE
Ceramic • Height: 1.4 m (4½ ft) • Archaic
• From Eleusis, Attica, Greece

ARCHAEOLOGICAL MUSEUM
OF ELEUSIS, GREECE

This neck-handled amphora is
the name vase of the Polyphemus
Painter. It ended its use-life as a
funerary urn for a boy of about ten
years of age, and today it is among
the finest vessels known from the
period. The neck depicts the blinding
of the inebriated cyclops Polyphemus
by the hero Odysseus (in white)
in a scene that references Homer's
Odyssey. On the body, a series of
uniquely large figures portrays
the escape of Perseus from the
sisters of the gorgon Medusa
in the moments after her
beheading. Both scenes may
have been chosen by the artist
deliberately as an analogy for
death, or for escape from it.

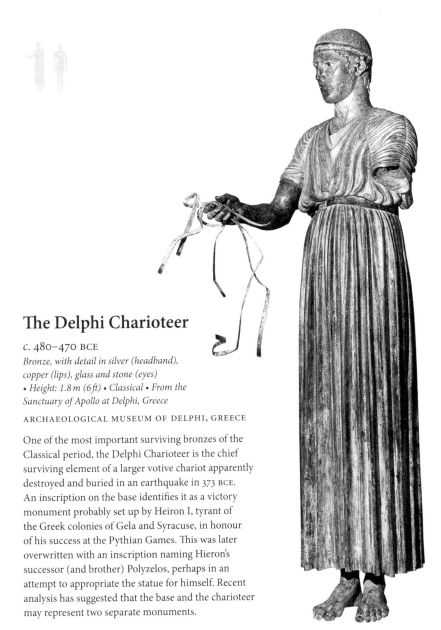

The Delphi Charioteer

c. 480–470 BCE

Bronze, with detail in silver (headband), copper (lips), glass and stone (eyes)
• Height: 1.8 m (6 ft) • Classical • From the Sanctuary of Apollo at Delphi, Greece

ARCHAEOLOGICAL MUSEUM OF DELPHI, GREECE

One of the most important surviving bronzes of the Classical period, the Delphi Charioteer is the chief surviving element of a larger votive chariot apparently destroyed and buried in an earthquake in 373 BCE. An inscription on the base identifies it as a victory monument probably set up by Heiron I, tyrant of the Greek colonies of Gela and Syracuse, in honour of his success at the Pythian Games. This was later overwritten with an inscription naming Hieron's successor (and brother) Polyzelos, perhaps in an attempt to appropriate the statue for himself. Recent analysis has suggested that the base and the charioteer may represent two separate monuments.

THE PARTHENON MARBLES

c. 447–433/2 BCE

*Marble • Height of metopes: 1.2 m (4 ft), height of
Figure G (far right), East Pediment: 1.7 m (5½ ft)
• Classical • From the Acropolis, Athens, Greece*

BRITISH MUSEUM, LONDON, UK

The Parthenon was built to house Pheidias'
monumental chryselephantine (gold and
ivory) statue of Athena. Surviving annual
accounts record its installation in *c.* 438 BCE,
although, like Pheidias' Olympian Zeus,
the statue is now lost. It, like the decorative
scheme on the temple itself, was a tour de
force of Athenian propaganda. The ninety-two
metopes (sculptural panels) that made up
the exterior Doric frieze all depicted scenes
of mythical battle: Lapiths versus Centaurs
(Centauromachy) on the south, Greeks
versus Amazons (Amazonomachy) on the
west, gods versus giants (Gigantomachy) on
the east and the Sack of Troy (Iliupersis)
on the north. All share the common theme

of Athenian victory over non-Greeks, of
civilization over barbarism. The 160 m
(525 ft) long inner Ionic frieze is generally
identified as a depiction of the Panathenaic
procession to the Acropolis that, along with
musical and athletic events, formed part of
the city's most important religious festival.
It has been suggested that the scene includes
a veiled reference to the Athenian-led
victory against the Persians at Marathon.
The pedimental sculpture at the east, shown
here, depicts the mythical birth of Athena
from the head of Zeus, watched over by
the Olympian gods; those at the west depict
the battle between Athena and Poseidon for
the right to be patron deity of Athens.

This metope (South Metope XXX) derives from the Centauromachy, the battle between Lapiths and Centaurs at the wedding feast of the Lapith king Pirithous, and depicts a Centaur trampling a crouching Lapith, posed to strike.

The Riace Warriors

c. 460–450 BCE
Bronze, with detail in calcite (eyes), silver (teeth), copper (nipples and lips) • *Height Statue A: 2 m (6½ ft), Statue B: 2 m (6½ ft)* • *Classical* • *Recovered from the sea off Riace Marina, Reggio Calabria, Italy*

NATIONAL ARCHAEOLOGICAL MUSEUM
OF REGGIO CALABRIA, ITALY

The Riace Warriors were cast in sections using a complex technique known as the indirect lost-wax method. They probably formed part of a victory monument set up in a Greek sanctuary, lost when the transport ship removing them to Italy was wrecked, although their identity remains a matter of debate. The proportions and modelling of Statue A (left) suggest it may depict a hero, while Statue B (far left), reconstructed with a Corinthian helmet tipped back on the head, has been interpreted as a strategos (general). Some scholars have suggested a link, still unproven, with a monument of thirteen bronzes by the sculptor Pheidias erected at Delphi to commemorate the victory at Marathon.

Ivory heads

c. 340–330 BCE

Ivory • Height of 'Philip': 3.2 cm (1¼ in.), height of 'Alexander': 3.4 cm (1½ in.) • Classical • From Tomb II at Vergina, Imathia, Greece

MUSEUM OF THE ROYAL TOMBS
OF AIGAI, VERGINA, GREECE

An elaborate wooden kline (couch) accompanied Philip into his tomb. Relief elements of ivory, glass and gold were set on the front and legs; gilt-relief and paint covered the remainder. Two scenes can be distinguished. An assembly of the gods, including Aphrodite, Dionysus, Eros and Silenus, decorated the upper cross bar. Below this was a hunt scene including at least fourteen individualized figures, mounted and on foot. The two heads shown here derive from the latter. Originally brightly painted, they are commonly identified as Philip II (left) and Alexander the Great (right).

The Cup of Pheidias

c. 430–410 BCE

Ceramic • Height: 7.7 cm (3 in.) • Classical • From the Sanctuary of Zeus at Olympia, Greece

ARCHAEOLOGICAL MUSEUM
OF OLYMPIA, GREECE

Renowned in his own time as preeminent among sculptors, the Athenian Pheidias today occupies an exalted position in the history of Greek art. His portfolio was broad, although his colossal Zeus enthroned, created for the Olympian Temple of Zeus in *c.* 430 BCE, was his masterwork and came to be counted among the Seven Wonders of the Ancient World. A workshop located to the west of the temple is now identified as that in which Pheidias created the Zeus. As well as tools, moulds and raw materials, excavation yielded this small black-glazed cup bearing a graffito on the base that reads: 'Pheidio Eimi' or 'I belong to Pheidias'.

The Lekythos of Xenophantos

c. 400–380 BCE
Ceramic • Height: 38.5 cm (15¼ in.)
• Classical • From Kerch (ancient
Pantikapaion), Crimea

STATE HERMITAGE MUSEUM,
ST PETERSBURG, RUSSIA

This extraordinary squat lekythos (oil
flask) is the largest ever manufactured
and, in its use of red-figure technique,
mould-made relief, white-slip, painting
and gilding, is also perhaps the most
complex. This rare combination is
paralleled by a unique mixture of Greek
and Persianizing elements, and motifs
from myth and reality. The body
depicts Persians hunting boar, stag
and griffin. The location has been
suggested as the mythical land
of the Hyperboreans and the
entire composition as a Greek
reflection on Persian hubris
and territorial aspiration.
It is signed: 'Xenophantos
the Athenian made this.'

THE CHIGI VASE

c. 650–640 BCE

Ceramic • Height: 26 cm (10¼ in.) • Archaic • From a tomb at Monte Aguzzo, Veii, Etruria (Italy)

NATIONAL ETRUSCAN MUSEUM, VILLA GIULIA, ROME, ITALY

A masterpiece of Archaic art, this exquisite olpe (wine jug) provides perhaps the earliest artistic representation of the hoplite phalanx. Hoplites were not professional soldiers, but citizen farmers who fought around the agricultural calendar and took their name from the equipment they carried: (ta hopla), rather than, as is sometimes claimed, their shield, the aspis (often erroneously called the hoplon). During the Archaic period, there was no standard set of equipment. Instead, various elements of weaponry and armour were combined in lighter or heavier combinations. The earlier Archaic phalanx was probably a fairly loose arrangement, and the Spartan poet Tyrtaeus provides often rather bloody accounts of Archaic battle that suggest mobility and the use of mixed troop types.

By the Classical period, the phalanx had evolved into a tightly ranked formation in which the thrusting spear was the primary weapon and the shield was carried so as to protect the right flank of the man to the left. The ideology of hoplite warfare played a major role in polis society, although how it worked in practice (including the reality of the othismos, or 'push', said to have occurred when two phalanxes met), and its social and political implications, remain a matter of debate.

Later written sources suggest that the advance of the phalanx was sounded by trumpet and that men would sing a hymn or paean to keep time and maintain formation. Spartans are recorded using flute players, as here, to the same end.

The Kouros of Kroisos

c. 530 BCE
*Marble • Height: 1.9 m (6¼ ft) • Archaic
• From Anavyssos, Attica, Greece*

NATIONAL ARCHAEOLOGICAL MUSEUM,
ATHENS, GREECE

This life-sized kouros (youth) was erected
as a marker above the grave of an Athenian
hoplite named Kroisos. Kouroi were not
intended to portray any one individual, but
rather an idealized version of youth that
embodied the aristocratic ideals of arete (a
complex concept often translated as 'virtue')
and kalokagathia (physical and moral
excellence). Like their female counterparts,
they marked an important step towards
sculptural realism, although the pose, as
here, was stiff and standardized: upright and
forward-facing with arms slightly flexed,
fists clenched and left leg forward. Its base
preserves an inscription inviting passersby
to: 'stay and mourn at the monument for
dead Kroisos whom violent Ares destroyed,
fighting in the front rank'.

The Helmet of Miltiades

c. 490 BCE

Bronze • Height (maximum): 28 cm (11 in.) • Archaic-Classical • From the Sanctuary of Zeus at Olympia, Greece

ARCHAEOLOGICAL MUSEUM OF OLYMPIA, GREECE

Normally cast in one piece, the Corinthian helmet offered full-head protection, albeit at a cost to vision and hearing. It was, as a result, the most popular type throughout the Archaic and earlier Classical period and is closely associated with the emergence of hoplite warfare. Weapons and armour, often the spoils of war, were a common offering within the Panhellenic sanctuaries of the Greek mainland. This helmet bears an extraordinary inscription to Zeus that identifies its dedicator as Miltiades, likely the Athenian general responsible for the Greek victory against the Persians at the Battle of Marathon in 490 BCE.

The Serpent Column

c. 479 BCE

Bronze • Height of column: 5.4 m (17¾ ft)
• Classical • From the Sanctuary of Apollo
at Delphi, Greece

ISTANBUL HIPPODROME (COLUMN);
ISTANBUL ARCHAEOLOGICAL MUSEUMS,
TURKEY (HEAD)

The Serpent Column was erected at Delphi
by the Greek veterans of the Battle of Plataea
(479 BCE) to commemorate the Greek victory
that ended the Second Persian War.
Purportedly manufactured from the spoils
of the battle, and inscribed with the names
of the thirty-one city-states that fought, it
originally stood approximately 9 m (29½ ft)
tall and took the form of three entwined
snakes, the heads of which supported a
monumental gold tripod bowl. The bowl
was stolen in the 4th century BCE but the
column survived until the 4th century CE,
when it was moved to Constantinople by
the Emperor Constantine and erected on
the spina (spine) of the ancient hippodrome.

The Lenormant Relief

c. 410 BCE

*Marble • Height: 39 cm (15¼ in.),
width: 52 cm (20½ in.) • Classical
• From the Acropolis, Athens, Greece*

ACROPOLIS MUSEUM,
ATHENS, GREECE

Named for its three banks of rowers, the development of the trireme at Athens during the 6th century BCE revolutionized naval warfare and underpinned Athenian superiority across the Mediterranean into the Classical period. At its peak, the Athenian navy comprised some 400 ships, and excavations at the port of Piraeus have revealed the sheds in which the fleet was overwintered. No wreck has ever been located and therefore contemporary texts and artistic depictions are vital for understanding their construction. This small, shallow relief depicts the starboard midships of a trireme under oar, perhaps the Athenian state ship *Paralos* carrying the hero after whom it was named.

Prow ram

c. 490–323 BCE
Bronze • Length: 80 cm (31½ in.) • Classical • Provenance unknown (said to be from Artemision, Euboea, Greece)
ARCHAEOLOGICAL MUSEUM OF PIRAEUS,
ATHENS, GREECE

The prow-mounted ram was the principal offensive weapon of the trireme. It was designed to break the hull of an enemy vessel at vulnerable points amidships, or else at the stern having broken through the enemy line. The ram might equally serve to shear the oar banks, although the manoeuvre was not without considerable risk. Very few examples of prow rams are known to exist. When not captured or lost, the Piraeus Naval Inventories (see opposite) suggest that the rams of decommissioned ships were reassigned, while damaged examples could be sold for scrap.

Marble eye

c. 500–400 BCE

Marble • Height: 24 cm (9½ in.), length: 53 cm (20¾ in.)
• Archaic-Classical • From Zea Harbour, Piraeus, Greece

ARCHAEOLOGICAL MUSEUM OF PIRAEUS,
ATHENS, GREECE

This ophthalmos (eye) is one of a pair that once
decorated the bow of an Athenian trireme. It is likely
that it was among provisions stored within the ship
sheds of Zea Harbour or its associated arsenals.
Ophthalmoi are included among inventories of naval
equipment preserved on a series of 4th-century BCE stelai
known collectively as the Piraeus Naval Inventories,
as are named ships (*Wind-Loving, Immortal*) and their
condition, including several for which these eyes are
listed as broken or missing. This example includes
eyelids and a sculpted tear duct and preserves traces
of its painted iris. Ophthalmoi played on the idea of
the trireme as a charging animal, but may also have
been considered to protect the ship from evil.

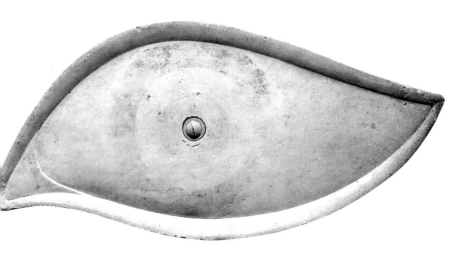

Cuirass

c. 400–336 BCE

Iron and gold • Dimensions: unknown
• Classical • From Tomb II at Vergina,
Imathia, Greece

MUSEUM OF THE ROYAL TOMBS
OF AIGAI, VERGINA GREECE

This iron cuirass, the oldest of its type, was part
of a ceremonial panoply that accompanied
Phillip II to the grave. It is formed of hinged
plates, leather-lined and edged with gold
bands bearing a Lesbian cymation. Eight
gold lion heads adorned the chestplate and
left side; gold rings guided leather thongs,
which fixed the plates in place. A gold
panel on the right side depicted Athena,
while further panels with palmette motifs
decorated the leather pteruges (skirt), now
lost. Phillip's son, Alexander, appears in a
similar cuirass on the eponymous mosaic
from Pompeii (see page 253).

Projectile point

c. 350 BCE

Bronze • Length: 6.8 cm (2¾ in.) • Classical
• Provenance unknown (said to be from
Olynthus, Chalcidice, Greece)

ARTHUR M. SACKLER MUSEUM, HARVARD
ART MUSEUMS, CAMBRIDGE, USA

Philip II marched on Olynthus in 348 BCE.
The city was put to siege and, we are told,
eventually betrayed with its citizens sold
into slavery to recoup the cost of war.
This point bears a cast inscription in
retrograde: ΦΙΛΙΠΠΟ, 'of Philip'. Much
larger than a typical arrowhead, it may
have constituted artillery. The practice of
inscribing ammunition is also seen on the
lead bullets used by Macedonian slingers,
which commonly bore sardonic messages
for the recipient, including 'catch!'

The Stele of Dexileos

c. 394 BCE
Marble • Height: 1.9 m (6 ft) • Classical
• From the Kerameikos Cemetery, Athens, Greece
KERAMEIKOS MUSEUM, ATHENS, GREECE

A casualty of the Corinthian War between Sparta
and an Athenian-led coalition, Dexileos is named on
two other monuments at Athens. The first, a casualty
list for those 'who fell at Corinth' and the second, a
monument set up by the Hippeis (cavalry) to honour
those killed at the Battles of the Nemea River and
Koroneia. The dead man's family, however, paid
for a third, a cenotaph (empty tomb), which depicts
Dexileos as an individual and a hero, borrowing
the sort of imagery normally reserved for state
monuments such as the Parthenon. The inscription
reads: 'Dexileos, son of Lysanias, of Thorikos. He
was born in the archonship of Teisandros (414/3 BCE);
He died in that of Euboulides (394/3 BCE), at Corinth,
one of the five horsemen.'

Spear-butt

c. 500–400 BCE

Bronze • Length: 28.7 cm (11¼ in.) • Archaic-Classical • Provenance unknown (said to be from the Sanctuary of Zeus at Olympia, Greece)

BRITISH MUSEUM, LONDON, UK

The dory (spear) was the primary weapon of the hoplite. Measuring approximately 2.7 m (8¾ ft) in length, it was commonly provisioned with a solid-cast, four-sided, butt-spike known as a sauroter (literally 'lizard killer'), which served both to balance the weapon and to prevent the end of the shaft from splintering. It would have allowed the spear to stand unsupported and could be adapted as a back-up weapon in the event that the head was broken, although it is commonly represented in art and literature being used to deliver a *coup de grâce* to a downed enemy. The inscription on this example identifies it as a votive offering: 'Theodoros anetheke basileus', 'Theodoros dedicated me to [Zeus] the king.'

Casualty list

c. 500–400 BCE
Marble • Height: 24.1 cm (9½ in.) • Archaic-Classical • From the Agora, Athens, Greece
MUSEUM OF THE ANCIENT AGORA,
ATHENS, GREECE

Following their cremation and collective burial, the war dead of 5th-century BCE Athens (including slaves and foreigners) were memorialized on stelai erected in the state cemetery and in commemorative orations delivered annually during wartime. Given the more common practice of cremating and burying the dead on the battlefield, Athens' treatment of its sons was highly unusual. These deliberately modest casualty lists were designed to reinforce the collective, democratic identity of those who had died fighting for the polis, organizing the citizen dead by tribal affiliation, recording names (although not patronymics), locations and only occasionally military rank.

Gorytos

400–336 BCE
Silver and gold • Height (maximum): 46.5 cm (18¼ in.),
width (maximum): 25.5 cm (10 in.) • Classical • From
Tomb II at Vergina, Imathia, Greece

MUSEUM OF THE ROYAL TOMBS OF AIGAI,
VERGINA, GREECE

When excavated, this silver-gilt gorytos (quiver
and bow case) was found with a full set of seventy-
four arrows, of three different calibres. It is of a
type used by the Scythians of the Eurasian steppe,
a group renowned in antiquity for their skill
with a recurve bow. Narrative decoration in
repoussé depicts the capture of a city. Attackers
are shown defiling the urban sanctuaries in which
the citizenry had sought shelter; defenders are
depicted unsuccessfully attempting to respond
to the onslaught while women flee with babes
in arms. The identity of the woman with whom
this gorytos was buried has been much debated,
although she may have been Philip II's sixth wife,
the Getic-Scythian princess, Meda.

Spartan shield

c. 425 BCE

Bronze • Diameter: 97 cm (38¼ in.)
• Classical • From the Agora,
Athens, Greece

MUSEUM OF THE ANCIENT
AGORA, ATHENS, GREECE

According to Pausanias, the Stoa Poikile (Painted Stoa) in the Athenian Agora was decorated with scenes of Athenian military victory, rendered by some of the most renowned artists of the Classical period: Polygnotos' *Sack of Troy,* Mikon's *Amazonomachy,* Panainos' famous *Battle of Marathon* and an unattributed depiction of the *Battle of Oinoēa.* It also held Athenian spoils. This shield, one of a group also recorded by Pausanias, preserves a punched inscription that identifies it as one of several taken from the Spartans following their surrender at the Battle of Sphakteria (425 BCE): 'The Athenians [took this] from the Lakedaimonians at Pylos.'

Boeotian helmet

c. 400–323 BCE
Bronze • Height: 24 cm (9½ in.), depth: 34 cm
(13¼ in.) • Classical • Found in the River Tigris, Iraq

ASHMOLEAN MUSEUM, OXFORD, UK

In the spring of 334 BCE, Alexander the Great led
an army of between 30,000 and 50,000 soldiers
into Asia. This force crossed the Tigris in 331 BCE,
marching north towards what would be a decisive
victory over the Persian Achaemenid Empire
at Gaugamela (traditionally located near the
modern city of Mosul). According to the historian
Diodorus Siculus, the crossing was difficult and
part of Alexander's army was lost to the current.
It is not impossible that this helmet belonged
to a cavalryman who lost his equipment,
or perhaps even his life, during this
episode, although the type
continued in use during
the Hellenistic period.

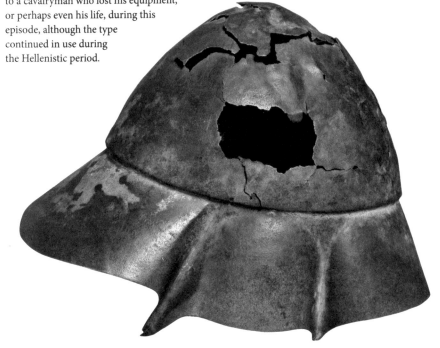

The Naxian Sphinx

c. 570–560 BCE
*Marble • Height: 2.9 m (9½ ft) • Archaic • From
the Sanctuary of Apollo at Delphi, Greece*
ARCHAEOLOGICAL MUSEUM
OF DELPHI, GREECE

Representing the first dedication at Delphi by an
Aegean island, this sphinx was set up by the elite
of Naxos in *c.* 570 BCE, during a period that saw
a monumentalization of the sanctuary itself and,
perhaps, the foundation of the Panhellenic Pythian
Games. It originally sat atop a huge Ionic column
at a total height of more than 12 m (39¼ ft). The use
of a column to, literally, place one's votive above all
others would quickly be copied. The human-animal
hybrid was a favoured Naxian motif, and its height
and its careful choice of location within the sanctuary
served to reinforce both its visual and ideological
impact and the power and influence of its dedicants.

The Nikandre Kore

c. 650 BCE

Marble • Height: 1.7 m (5¾ ft) • Archaic • From the Sanctuary of Artemis and Apollo at Delos, Greece

NATIONAL ARCHAEOLOGICAL MUSEUM, ATHENS, GREECE

This life-sized kore (maiden) is the earliest complete example of female statuary in Greek art. She marks a shift towards the sculptural use of marble and, like other Archaic korai and kouroi, a Daedalic style represented by full-frontal perspective, wig-like hair, large almond-shaped eyes and the enigmatic 'Archaic smile'. Set up close to the Temple of Artemis, the surviving inscription identifies the statue as a votive dedication to the goddess by Nikandre: 'Nikandre dedicated me to the far-shooter of arrows, the excellent daughter of Deinodikes of Naxos, the sister of Deinomenes, and the wife of Phraxos.'

The Peplophoros

c. 530 BCE

Marble • Height: 1.2 m (3¾ ft) • Archaic
• From the Acropolis, Athens, Greece

ACROPOLIS MUSEUM, ATHENS, GREECE

This Peplophoros stood on the Acropolis
alongside many of the most famous
examples of Archaic statuary. She is
named for her garment, not actually a
peplos but an ependytes (divine robe),
which preserves traces of brightly
coloured decoration. Far from the pure
white marble held in such high regard by
Neoclassical artists, most Greek sculpture
would have been painted and repainted,
perhaps even gaudily so to modern
sensibilities, using mineral pigments and
an organic binding agent (perhaps egg
or wax). Other korai show evidence of
gilding. This example was augmented
with bronze accoutrements, now lost,
and may have held a bow and a lance
or a pair of arrows, thereby identifying
her as either Artemis or Athena.

The Derveni Krater

c. 370 BCE

Bronze and silver • Height: 90.5 cm (35½ in.) • Classical
• From tomb B at Derveni, near Thessaloniki, Greece

ARCHAEOLOGICAL MUSEUM OF
THESSALONIKI, GREECE

The volute krater was normally used for the mixing
of wine and water at the symposion (drinking party),
although the elaborate Derveni Krater may have been
manufactured originally for use in Dionysian ritual
and, having lost its stand, ended its life as a cinerary
urn, in *c.* 330–300 BCE. The principal scene on the
body depicts the wedding of Dionysus and Ariadne,
although the composition as a whole may reference
death and rebirth. An inscription in silver letters on
the rim records: 'Astion, son of Anaxagoras, from the
city of Larissa', although it is unclear whether his were
the remains interred within. Despite its appearance,
the krater is not gold, but tin-copper bronze, with an
unusually high tin content of almost 15 per cent.

Artemis and Apollo

c. 600-500 BCE

Gold, ivory, silver and enamel • Height of 'Artemis' head: 23 cm (9 in.), height of 'Apollo' head: 24.5 cm (9½ in.) • Archaic • From the Sanctuary of Apollo at Delphi, Greece

ARCHAEOLOGICAL MUSEUM OF DELPHI, GREECE

The chryselephantine (gold and ivory) Apollo (opposite) and Artemis (above), as well as a further life-sized female identified as their mother, Leto, were recovered among a cache of valuable objects deposited in two pits beneath the later Sacred Way at Delphi. Burned and badly damaged, they perhaps represent the contents of a polis treasury, destroyed during a late 5th-century BCE conflagration and subsequently buried. Chryselephantine statuary was exceptionally expensive and technically challenging. Some scholars have attempted to link the figures with dedications made at Delphi by the Lydian king Croesus, while others have suggested they may have been offered by a tyrant of Samos.

Pitsa panels

c. 540–530 BCE
Wood • Height: 15 cm (6 in.),
width: 30 cm (11¾ in.) • Archaic
• From the Pitsa Cave, near Sikyon, Greece

NATIONAL ARCHAEOLOGICAL MUSEUM,
ATHENS, GREECE

Both wall and panel paintings were highly regarded in antiquity, although almost without exception those of which we know today are attested only by description or derivation. The four votive panels from the nymphaeum at Pitsa represent the earliest surviving examples in Greece. Painted in egg tempera, they employ the standard four-colour (tetrachrome) Archaic palette, but also use a great variety of mineral pigments, including cinnabar and pararealgar. The miniature scenes themselves are religious. This, the best preserved, was dedicated by two women – Euthydika and Eucholis – and depicts three women, three children and a man pouring libations in advance of animal sacrifice.

Cast votives

c. 650–500 BCE

Lead • Height of horse: 2.4 cm (1 in.), female: 3.5 cm (1½ in.), warrior: 3.5 cm (1½ in.), winged goddess: 3.5 cm (1½ in.) • Archaic • From the Sanctuary of Artemis Orthia, Sparta, Greece

FITZWILLIAM MUSEUM, CAMBRIDGE, UK

The Sanctuary of Artemis Orthia at Sparta was probably established during the 9th century BCE, although it received its first monumental temple during the Archaic period. The cult associated the two goddesses Artemis and Orthia, whose attributes mirrored contemporary Spartan concerns of fertility and the protection and education of its children. The poet Alcman provides some evidence for the nature of Archaic cultic ritual, and a prominence for women that reflected their freedoms within wider Spartan society. More than 100,000 of these votives have been recovered from the sanctuary: inexpensive offerings for visiting dedicants in a range of shapes, including deities, warriors, animals, wreaths and garments.

Votive mask

c. 600–500 BCE
Terracotta • Dimensions: unknown • Archaic • From the Sanctuary of Artemis Orthia, Sparta, Greece
ARCHAEOLOGICAL MUSEUM OF SPARTA, GREECE

Hundreds of intact or nearly intact mould-made terracotta masks and several thousand additional fragments have been excavated from the Sanctuary of Artemis Orthia. This collection incorporates seven broad types, including warriors, gorgoneia and, as here, the elderly. Not all of the masks are life-sized and some lack certain facial features. As such, it is unlikely they were worn. It has been suggested that they represent models of perishable originals, perhaps linen or wood, which would have been utilized for dance and ritual within the sanctuary. Their use here has been considered a link between ritual drama and theatrical performance.

Illyrian helmet and death mask

c. 520 BCE
Bronze and gold • Height: 22 cm (8¾ in.), diameter: 20.5 cm (8 in.) • Archaic • From tomb 115 at the cemetery of Sindos, Chalkidiki, Greece
ARCHAEOLOGICAL MUSEUM OF THESSALONIKI, GREECE

As with other aspects of Macedonian culture, Archaic burial practices were markedly different to those seen further south. As Athens and other poleis turned towards the sanctuary as the primary arena for conspicuous display, the elite of Macedon continued to embrace the cemetery. As such, females continued to be buried with opulent grave goods and male 'warrior burial' survived far later here than elsewhere in Greece. The extraordinary precious-metal wealth of the region influenced Macedonian art, economy and politics. Gold, some of it perhaps panned from the Gallikos River, was used at Sindos for inlay, jewelry and, in a handful of cases, repoussé masks, such as this.

FUNERAL AND RITUAL 225

The Tomb of the Diver

c. 470 BCE

Poros limestone • Length of cover slab: 2.2 m (7¼ ft), width of cover slab: 1.1 m (3½ ft) • Classical • From Paestum, Italy

NATIONAL ARCHAEOLOGICAL MUSEUM OF PAESTUM, ITALY

The Tomb of the Diver is one of only two examples of Archaic or Classical monumental painting to have survived intact. Executed in true fresco (using a pigment mixture on wet plaster), the interior face of the cover slab depicts a nude diver descending to an inlet or stream. Unique in Greek art, the dive has recently been argued to represent death, and the scene itself the promise of safety awaiting at the shore beyond. The four walls of the tomb depict a symposion (drinking party), and place the dead man (literally) at the centre of revelry destined to last for eternity. The shell of a tortoise accompanied the body, perhaps the remains of a lyre included to allow him to perform.

Articulated female figurine

c. 500–400 BCE
Terracotta • Height: 12 cm (4¾ in.)
• Archaic-Classical • Provenance unknown

METROPOLITAN MUSEUM
OF ART, NEW YORK CITY, USA

Although often referred to as dolls, the articulated female figurines of the Archaic and Classical periods served a much wider range of functions than as a simple child's plaything. This mould-made example wears a short garment known as a chitoniskos (little chiton) and a polos headdress, and may represent a ritual dancer associated with fertility cult and marriage. They may have served as votive nymphai (brides), dedicated by young women preparing for adulthood. As offerings in graves they may have possessed an additional chthonic symbolism or, where pierced and threaded (as in this example), they may have been hung, or worn, as a device to ward off evil.

227

ROYAL TOMBS OF AIGAI

c. 340–300 BCE

Limestone • Dimensions: unknown • Classical-Hellenistic • From Vergina, Imathia, Greece
MUSEUM OF THE ROYAL TOMBS OF AIGAI, VERGINA, GREECE

Buried beneath a tumulus approximately 110 m (361 ft) in diameter and 13 m (43 ft) high, the royal burial cluster comprises four tombs and a heroön (a shrine to the heroic dead). The Tomb of the Freestanding Columns has been all but destroyed. The smallest of the surviving group, a looted cist known as the Tomb of Persephone, contained the scattered remains of a man,

woman and as many as five infants. It preserves some of the most important fresco work of the Hellenistic period. Perhaps by Nikomachos of Thebes, an abduction scene adorned the north wall, a mourning Demeter adorned the east, and the three Fates – Clotho, Lachesis and Atropos – adorned the south. A chariot scene decorated the antechamber of the

The cremated remains of Philip were perhaps washed with wine before being wrapped in an elaborate gold thread and purple cloth and interred in this solid gold larnax (cinerary chest). Weighing approximately 8 kg (17¾ lb), the lid is embossed with the so-called Macedonian Sun, today a contentious political symbol.

Tomb of the Prince. The undecorated main chamber held the cremated remains of a fourteen-year-old male, wrapped, placed in a silver hydria (water jar) and set into a platform. Tomb II is identified as that of Philip II and Meda, whose cremated remains were interred in respective gold larnakes in the main chamber and anti-chamber. Both it and the Tomb of the Prince are barrel-vaulted

chamber tombs of Macedonian type. Their facades are ornamented with plasterwork in imitation of Doric architecture. A pair of relief shields flank the monumental marble doorway of the Tomb of the Prince, while the facade of Tomb II incorporates two end pillars, two Doric half-columns and an exquisite painted hunt frieze in which both Philip and Alexander have been identified.

Innovation and Adaptation

The Nike of Samothrace overlooked the theatre of the Sanctuary of the Great Gods at Samothrace. She stands atop the prow of a ship and may have been set up by Rhodes in commemoration of a naval victory at Side in 190 BCE.

The late Classical victory of Philip II at the Battle of Chaeronea in 338 BCE heralded the submission of Greece (with the exception of Sparta) beneath Macedonian hegemony. With stability on the mainland, the king turned his attention to the East. Philip, however, was assassinated by his bodyguard at Aigai in 336 BCE, leaving his son, Alexander III, to fulfil his father's ambitions. Alexander's Asian expedition extended Greek influence further east than ever before. His victory at Issus provided him with control of southern Asia Minor; in 332 BCE, Tyre in Egypt fell after a six-month siege; in 331 BCE, his defeat of Darius III at Gaugamela (Arbela, near Mosul, Iraq) resulted in the collapse of the Achaemenid Empire and extended the Macedonian Empire as far as the Indus River. He pushed through the province of Bactria-Sogdiana in 329 BCE and in 326 BCE won his last major victory against the Hindu King Porus at the Hydaspes River in modern Pakistan. His expansionist ambitions were apparently only halted by mutiny at the Hyphasis; his men, evidently, were less ambitious than he was.

Alexander's death in 323 BCE marked the beginning of the Hellenistic period and a series of internal conflicts were triggered as his former generals and close companions moved to carve up the dead king's empire. These were the so-called Wars of the *Diadochoi* or 'successors' and, interspersed with various diplomatic agreements, several major battles and a significant dose of political Machiavellianism, they forced a fundamental change in what it meant to be Greek. From these conflicts, three royal houses emerged: the Ptolemaic in Egypt, the Antigonid in Macedonia and the Seleucid in Asia. These were later augmented by the Greco-Bactrian Kingdom and the Indo-Greek Kingdom. This was the political framework in which Hellenistic material culture developed. The result was the formation of hybrid cultures, neither Greek nor indigenous, but something new, and a situation in which many of the most significant developments of the period took place beyond mainland Greece.

There was continuity between Classical and Hellenistic material culture, although Classical Greek forms and motifs were adapted to suit local styles and contexts. Sanctuaries, and their festivals, continued to be patronised and monuments continued to be built. In architecture, however, there was a shift away from the Doric order, long-favoured for temples and secular public buildings, and an increased visibility of evermore elaborate Ionic architecture and the exterior use of the Corinthian order. First identified on the Late Classical Choragic Monument of Lysikrates at Athens, and combined with Ionic elements in the Propylon of Ptolemy II at Samothrace, *c.* 280 BCE, it was during the 2nd century BCE that the potential of the Corinthian order began to be fully realized. Sculpture embraces naturalism and realism, led by Lysippos and exemplified in works like Polyeuktos's Demosthenes (*c.* 280 BCE). At Pergamon, works such as the Dying Gaul (mid 3rd century BCE) and the gigantomachy of the later Great Altar of Zeus reflect the development of the Baroque style. In theatre, a

This cast bronze plaque depicts a human head at the centre of a crescent moon. Recovered from the Temple of the Indented Niches at Ai Khanoum, it may reflect the worship of a moon cult within the city.

reduction in freedom of speech saw the New Comedy move away from Classical political satire towards safer subject matter and the use of stock characters.

There were advances in science and astronomy under the likes of Archimedes of Syracuse, Aristarchus of Samos and Eratosthenes of Cyrene, while several major philosophical schools emerged in the wake of prominent philosophers. Sceptics, allegedly founded by Pyrrho of Elis, questioned the reality of absolute truth and the indeterminable nature of things; rational virtue was propounded by the Stoic School, founded by Zeno (originally a Cynic) *c.* 300 BCE, and a life of quiet pleasure by the Epicurean School founded in *c.* 307 BCE. During the early 3rd century BCE, one member of Aristotle's Peripatetic School is attested at Ai Khanoum in Afghanistan, having travelled there with a copy of maxims, or moral guidelines, brought from the Oracle at Delphi.

From the 2nd century BCE onwards, there is an increasing Roman influence visible in Greece. Corinth was sacked by Mummius in 146 BCE and Athens was captured by Sulla in 86 BCE. In the aftermath of the Battle of Actium in 31 BCE and with the death of Cleopatra VII, the last Ptolemaic ruler, in 30 BCE, the Hellenistic period drew to a close and Greece finally became the subject of Roman rule.

The Temple of Apollo at Didyma is one of the most important of the Hellenistic period. Envisaged as a replacement for its destroyed Archaic predecessor, work was begun in c. 300 BCE and continued for more than a century, although the temple was never completed.

Figurine of a comic actor

c. 320 BCE
Terracotta • Height: 13 cm (5 in.)
• Hellenistic • Provenance unknown
(said to be from Piraeus, Greece)

BRITISH MUSEUM,
LONDON, UK

Terracotta masks and figurines make up the largest quantity of surviving theatre-related material, a product of the fact that the theatre was as popular among the poor as it was the rich. Comic figures are distinctive, offering information on costume and characterization, and the reception of certain groups within Hellenistic society. This example depicts a runaway slave. With trumpet-mouthed mask, padded belly and protruding leather phallus, he takes refuge on an altar, perhaps to avoid his master's anger.

Honorary decree

c. 300–250 BCE

*Bronze • Height: 54 cm (21¼ in.)
• Hellenistic • From the Sanctuary
of Zeus at Olympia, Greece*

NATIONAL ARCHAEOLOGICAL
MUSEUM, ATHENS, GREECE

The Olympiad remained popular into the Hellenistic period and both the athletic facilities at Olympia and the programme of the event itself continued to develop under Hellenistic patronage. This plaque preserves a proxeny decree by the Eleians in honour of Demokrates, a victorious Olympic wrestler from the northern Aegean island of Tenedos. It designates Demokrates as proxenos, a formal role in which he was expected to further Eleian interests in his own community, fulfilling a variety of obligations from the diplomatic to the commercial. As such, Demokrates was granted certain privileges, including the right to own land in Elis and exemption from tax.

Relief plaque depicting a playwright

c. 100 BCE–100 CE

Marble • Height: 48.5 cm (19 in.),
width: 59.5 cm (23½ in.) • Hellenistic
• Provenance unknown

PRINCETON UNIVERSITY ART
MUSEUM, USA

This plaque depicts the Greek Menander
(*c.* 341–292 BCE), famed playwright of the
so-called New Comedy, a genre that moved
away from the socio-political critique of
the Old and Middle Comedy to embrace
everyday concerns, such as love and money.
Author of more than one hundred plays,
only one, *Dyskolos* (The Grouch), survives
nearly complete. The New Comedy utilized
stock characters; here Menander is shown
contemplating the masks of three: the youth,
the maiden and the old man. The scroll on
the table suggests he has stopped writing to
seek inspiration.

The Parian Marble

after 264 BCE

Marble • Maximum height of Section A (above): 57 cm (22½ in.), Section B: 39 cm (15¼ in.) • Hellenistic • From Paros, Cyclades

SECTION A: ASHMOLEAN
MUSEUM, OXFORD, UK
SECTION B: ARCHAEOLOGICAL
MUSEUM OF PAROS, GREECE

Originally measuring approximately 2 m (6½ ft) in height, although now broken and incomplete, the Parian Marble or Marmor Parium is the earliest surviving Greek chronicle; a monumental stele compiled during the reign of Diognetus (264/3 BCE) and recording a selective history of major events from the time of Kekrops (*c.* 1581 BCE), first king of Athens, to the archonship of Euctemon (299/8 BCE). Including reference to events such as the Deucalion Flood (*c.* 1528 BCE) and the start of the Trojan War (*c.* 1218 BCE), its text weaves together history and myth. Many of its entries concern literary history and it has been suggested that the stele may once have been installed in a Parian shrine dedicated to the Greek lyrical poet Archilochus.

The Elgin Throne

. 300 BCE

Marble • Height: 81.5 cm (32 in.) • Hellenistic
• Provenance unknown (from Athens, Greece)

J. PAUL GETTY MUSEUM, MALIBU, USA

The original location of this ceremonial chair or throne
remains unclear, although it may have been part of the
prohedria, the front row of seating in a theatre – perhaps
even the Theatre of Dionysus in Athens – occupied by
civic officials or those considered to have provided a
service to the polis. A partial inscription on the upper
rim probably names the dedicator: Boethos. The body
of the throne is covered with figures in relief: a pair
of wreaths at the rear, Theseus striking down an
Amazon at the left and the Tyrannicides,
Harmodius and Aristogeiton, at the
right. The unifying theme is
one of Athenian freedom.

ANTIKYTHERA MECHANISM

c. 150–100 BCE

Bronze and wood • Height (restored): 34 cm (13¼ in.), width (restored): 18 cm (7 in.)
• Hellenistic • Recovered from the sea off the island of Antikythera, Greece

NATIONAL ARCHAEOLOGICAL MUSEUM, ATHENS, GREECE

The Antikythera Mechanism was an extraordinarily complex celestial calculator. Within its wooden frame, an intricate mechanism of at least thirty gears drove hands across multiple output dials to track solar, lunar and planetary cycles. Two principal dials on the front face tracked at least the position of the sun and the moon in relation to the zodiac and the Egyptian calendar on any given day; a rotating ball on the lunar pointer probably indicated the lunar phase. Inscriptions above and below provided an indexed list of annual astronomical events. Dials on the back face tracked the Metonic and Kallipic cycles,

the eclipse cycles (Saros and Exeligmos) and, remarkably, the Greek festival cycle. Inscriptions on the 'back cover' constitute an 'operating manual', while those on the 'front cover' provided information on the Synodic cycles of Mercury, Venus, Mars, Jupiter and Saturn. Nothing this complex would appear again until the Middle Ages. The identity of the astronomer who owned the mechanism and the workshop responsible for its manufacture remain a matter of debate. The Antikythera ship appears to have sailed from the eastern Aegean, perhaps en route to Italy, and some have posited a link with Rhodes, then home to the astronomer Hipparchus.

Found by divers in 1901, over eighty fragments make up the surviving portion of the Antikythera Mechanism.
Modern scanning technology has made it possible to reconstruct the mechanism and read its inscriptions.

Cylindrical polar sundial

before *c.* 145 BCE

Limestone • Height: 44.5 cm (17½ in.) • Hellenistic
• From the gymnasium at Ai Khanoum, Afghanistan

NATIONAL MUSEUM OF AFGHANISTAN,
KABUL, AFGHANISTAN

The Hellenistic period saw the development
of a variety of sundial types. This cylindrical
equatorial example is unique. The passage of
time was tracked by a bronze axial gnomon,
now lost, which cast a shadow across two sets
of hour lines within the cylinder. While Ai
Khanoum sits at a latitude of 37°, the hour lines
are calculated for 23°, perhaps in reference to
major astronomical centres at Syene (present-
day Aswan) in Egypt or Ujjain in India. It may
have served as a demonstration model for
astronomy lessons held in the gymnasium.

Hermaic pillar

c. 200–150 BCE

Limestone • Height: 77 cm (30¼ in.)
• Hellenistic • From the gymnasium
at Ai Khanoum, Afghanistan

NATIONAL MUSEUM OF AFGHANISTAN,
KABUL, AFGHANISTAN

The sculptural herm (a pillar with a
human bust) was closely lined with
the gymnasium. This figure has been
tentatively identified as one Stratos, whose
sons, Triballos and Stratos, are identified
at Ai Khanoum in a dedicatory inscription
to the patron gods of the gymnasium,
Herakles and Hermes. It is thought
that they financed the rebuilding of the
public gymnasium and their father
may have held office as gymnasiarch,
the directorial responsibilities of
which are preserved on a roughly
contemporary stele from Veroia,
Macedonia. The bronze rod once
held in his left hand and his fillet
crown perhaps served as symbols
of his position.

Head of a philosopher

c. 240 BCE
Bronze • Height: 29 cm
(11½ in.) • Hellenistic
• Recovered from the sea off the
island of Antikythera, Greece

NATIONAL
ARCHAEOLOGICAL
MUSEUM, ATHENS, GREECE

Alongside the Mechanism (see page 240), the Antikythera ship was carrying a wealth of other objects when it was lost during the 1st century BCE, from marble statuary to furniture and the personal effects of passengers or crew, some of whom went down with the ship and whose remains have since been recovered. Other fragments recovered alongside this head suggest that the figure wore a cloak-like himation, held a staff in his left hand and extended his right in oratory fashion. It probably represents a Cynic philosopher and is commonly identified as Bion of Borysthenes (*c.* 320–250 BCE).

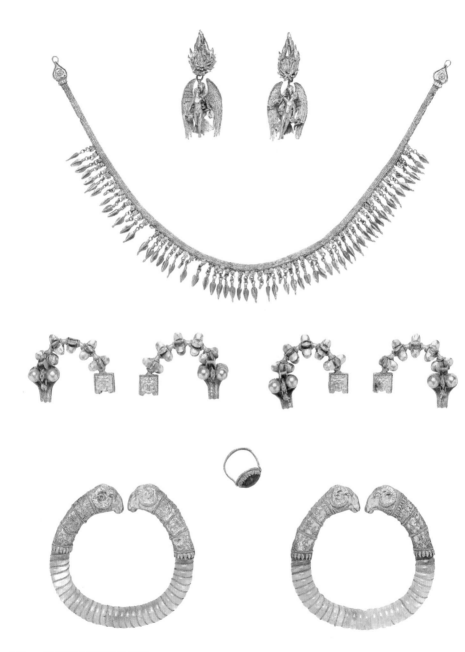

The Ganymede Jewelry

c. 300 BCE

Gold • Dimensions: various • Hellenistic • Provenance unknown (said to have been found near Thessaloniki, Greece)

METROPOLITAN MUSEUM OF ART,
NEW YORK CITY, USA

This exquisite jewelry group reflects the prosperity of Hellenistic Macedon and the artistic hybridity that accompanied the expansion of the Greek world under Alexander. It is named for two gold earrings depicting the Trojan prince Ganymede being carried off by Zeus in the guise of an eagle. The gold ring set with a cabochon emerald reflects a Hellenistic fashion for new precious and semi-precious stones made available by access to eastern trade routes, while the rock crystal bracelets with ram-head terminals reflect the popularity of matched bracelets after the Persian fashion.

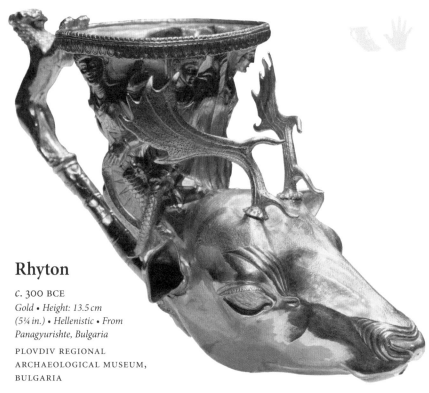

Rhyton

c. 300 BCE

Gold • Height: 13.5 cm
(5¼ in.) • Hellenistic • From
Panagyurishte, Bulgaria

PLOVDIV REGIONAL
ARCHAEOLOGICAL MUSEUM,
BULGARIA

This stag-shaped rhyton belongs to a
group of nine gold vessels collectively known as
the Panagyurishte Treasure. Together they manifest
Persian, Greek and Thracian artistic influences and may
have constituted a diplomatic gift from the *Diadochoi*
Lysimachus or Antigonus I Monophthalmus to a local
Thracian ruler, perhaps Seuthes III. Weight inscriptions
preserved on the group are cited as evidence for its
manufacture at Lampsakos in the northern Troad (present-
day northern Turkey). The handle of this rhyton terminates
in the form of a lion and a female head, while the body
depicts the Judgment of Paris, with dot-punched inscriptions
naming those involved: Paris, Hera, Athena and Aphrodite.

Loutrophoros

c. 320–300 BCE
Ceramic • Height: 78.7 cm (31 in.)
• Hellenistic • Provenance unknown
(said to be from Fasano, Puglia, Italy)

BRITISH MUSEUM, LONDON, UK

Named after the Apulian town where the
technique appears to have originated,
Gnathia ware was produced from *c.* 360 BCE,
and was arguably extinct by *c.* 250 BCE. Both
heavily exported and locally imitated, it
is characterized by the use of overpainted
polychromatic decoration on black glaze and
often incorporated vertical ribbing, as here.
This loutrophoros (water jar) is attributed
to one of the most important painters of the
style, the so-called Painter of the Louvre
Bottle. The body is decorated with painted
relief, a winged female adorns the cover
while its handle is modelled in the form
of a peacock standing within a yellow lotus.

Openwork hairnet

c. 300–200 BCE

Gold • Diameter: 23 cm (9 in.), diameter of medallion: 11.4 cm (4½ in.)
• Hellenistic • Provenance unknown (said to be from Karpenissi, Greece)

NATIONAL ARCHAEOLOGICAL MUSEUM, ATHENS, GREECE

Hellenistic women utilized a variety of hair accessories, including
sakkoi (bags), mitrai (turbans) and kekryphaloi (hairnets). Their
function was not simply aesthetic. Hair was implicitly linked to
feminine sexuality, and to keep one's hair in order showed both
awareness and acceptance of social convention. Nevertheless, dress
was an important element in female public performance, and even
hair accessories could be elaborate. The medallion of this example,
most likely a kekryphalos, is decorated in repoussé with a bust of
Artemis, framed by concentric bands separated by beaded wire and
filled with decorative motifs, semi-precious stones and green paste.

Statue of Ptolemy I

c. 300 BCE

Black basalt • Height: 64 cm (25¼ in.)
• Hellenistic • Provenance unknown
(said to be from the Nile Delta, Egypt)

BRITISH MUSEUM, LONDON, UK

Purportedly found in the lining of a well, this
statue probably depicts Ptolemy I, his royal
and divine authority signified by his nemes
headdress and uraeus. Ptolemy I was
a veteran of Alexander's campaigns in
the East and, in the aftermath of his
death, fought a protracted conflict
with the other successors to carve
up his empire. Ptolemy assumed the
office of satrap (provincial governor) of
Egypt on Alexander's death; in 305 BCE,
he took the title of Pharaoh, thereby
establishing the Ptolemaic Dynasty.

The Alexander Mosaic

c. 120–100 BCE

Marble • Height (including border):
3.1 m (10¼ ft), width: 5.8 m (19 ft),
• Hellenistic/Late Republic • From the
House of the Faun, Pompeii, Italy

NAPLES NATIONAL
ARCHAEOLOGICAL MUSEUM, ITALY

The Alexander Mosaic decorated the
floor of an exedra in one of the finest
houses at Pompeii, a commission
made in line with the aristocratic
Roman fashion for Greek art.
Incorporating around 1,500,000
tesserae, it is likely that it reproduces
a monumental Greek painting of
the late 4th century BCE, the setting
of which may very well have been
palatial. The subject is commonly
thought to be the Battle of Issus
(333 BCE), a victory that delivered
Alexander control of southern Asia
Minor. The Greek king is visible astride
his horse, presumably Bucephalus, in
the left foreground, while the Persian
king Darius III, from his chariot,
right of centre, gestures towards him,
anguished at the death of his soldier
beneath Alexander's spear.

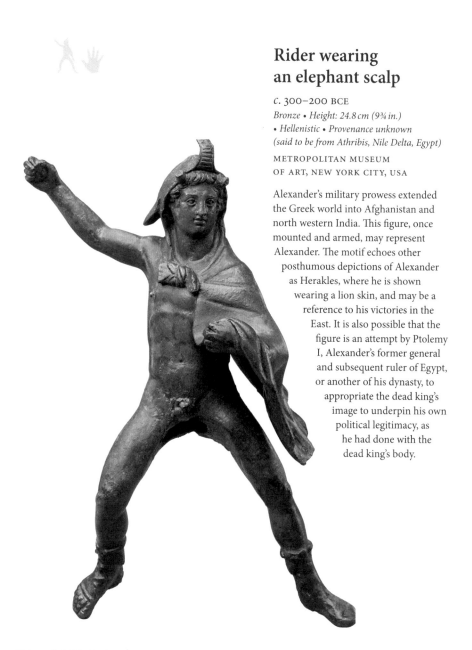

Rider wearing an elephant scalp

c. 300–200 BCE
Bronze • Height: 24.8 cm (9¾ in.)
• Hellenistic • Provenance unknown
(said to be from Athribis, Nile Delta, Egypt)

METROPOLITAN MUSEUM
OF ART, NEW YORK CITY, USA

Alexander's military prowess extended
the Greek world into Afghanistan and
north western India. This figure, once
mounted and armed, may represent
Alexander. The motif echoes other
posthumous depictions of Alexander
as Herakles, where he is shown
wearing a lion skin, and may be a
reference to his victories in the
East. It is also possible that the
figure is an attempt by Ptolemy
I, Alexander's former general
and subsequent ruler of Egypt,
or another of his dynasty, to
appropriate the dead king's
image to underpin his own
political legitimacy, as
he had done with the
dead king's body.

Model of a war elephant

c. 200–150 BCE

Terracotta • Height: 11.2 cm (4½ in.) • Hellenistic • From the necropolis of Myrina, Lemnos, Greece

LOUVRE, PARIS, FRANCE

Heavy war elephants were brought into the Greek military under Alexander, and continued to be used by his successors in the East. The shielded carrying tower would have housed a small number of troops armed with ranged weapons; a heavy caparison (cloth) would have offered some protection for the animal's flanks, while armour protected critical areas on the legs and neck. This elephant is shown trampling a Galatian warrior, and probably references the victories of Attalos I against the Tolistoagii or Tektosages in the Galatian War that delivered him the kingship and which were commemorated with monuments in the Sanctuary of Athena at Pergamon.

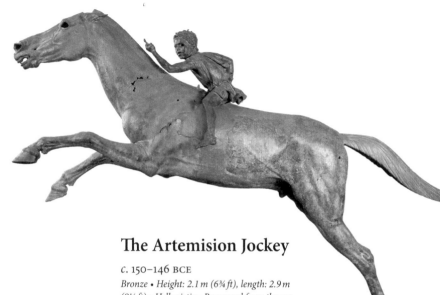

The Artemision Jockey

c. 150–146 BCE
Bronze • Height: 2.1 m (6¾ ft), length: 2.9 m
(9½ ft) • Hellenistic • Recovered from the sea
off Cape Artemision, Euboea, Greece

NATIONAL ARCHAEOLOGICAL MUSEUM,
ATHENS, GREECE

Part of a Hellenistic cargo that included the
Artemision Zeus, the Artemision Jockey depicts a
young African boy (perhaps a professional jockey)
seated on a horse at mid-gallop, looking over his
shoulder as he drives the animal onwards with a whip
or goad, now lost. A development out of the earlier
chariot and equestrian repertoire, and the earliest
example of a racehorse in action, it was perhaps a
victory monument set up in a sanctuary by a wealthy
Greek owner following success in the keles (single
horse race). It may represent one of the works looted
from Corinth by the Roman general Lucius Mummius
in 146 BCE, and was perhaps en route to Pergamon
as a gift for Attalos II when it was lost.

The Victorious Youth

c. 300–100 BCE
Bronze • Height: 1.5 m (5 ft) • Hellenistic
• Recovered from the sea off Fano on
the Adriatic Coast, Italy

J. PAUL GETTY MUSEUM, MALIBU, USA

The olive wreath worn by the Victorious
Youth identifies him as victor in an
athletic competition, an example of a
popular honorific type known as the
autostephanoumenos (self-crowning
athlete). He may once have held a palm
frond, an attribute awarded by the judges
at Olympia and Nemea. It is entirely
possible that it was from Olympia that
he was stolen in antiquity. Damage to the
lower legs probably occurred during the
separation of the statue from its base.
It remains the subject of a legally complex
restitution battle.

The Venus de Milo

C. 150–50 BCE
*Marble • Height: 2 m (6½ ft) • Hellenistic
• From Tramythia, Melos, Cyclades*
LOUVRE, PARIS, FRANCE

One of the most significant developments
of Hellenistic art, the female nude was
entirely a result of the cultural situation
in which it emerged. The Hellenistic
East offered greater public freedoms
for women and many Asian cultures
offered no taboo on female nudity,
while Hellenistic monarchies increased
the visibility of female royalty and
reduced the importance of the male
citizen. This Aphrodite stood in the civic
gymnasium on Melos, perhaps in her role
as a protector of young men. Surviving
fragments of her arms suggest she held an
apple in her left hand and gestured to it
with her right, and was thus represented
as the victor of the Judgement of Paris.

Canosa Group glassware

c. 225–200 BCE

Glass • Height of chalice: 11.1 cm (4¼ in.), height of sandwich glass bowl: 12 cm (4¾ in.), height of bossed bowl: 9 cm (3½ in.) • Hellenistic • Provenance unknown (said to be from a tomb at Canosa di Puglia, Apulia, Italy)

BRITISH MUSEUM, LONDON, UK

Although glass vessels were known in the Greek world during the Classical period, the scale of production increased dramatically during the Hellenistic period. These vessels belong to a larger group of high-quality clear-glass shapes favoured by, and buried with, the local elites of Canosa, southern Italy. They provide some of the earliest evidence for the manufacture of complete glass dining sets, as well as for the use of sandwich-gold glass, formed through the introduction of delicate gold-leaf motifs between two cast glass layers. They were almost certainly imported, perhaps from workshops in the eastern Mediterranean.

Name Vase of the Baltimore Painter

c. 320–310 BCE
Ceramic • Height: 1.1 m (3¾ ft) • Hellenistic
• Provenance unknown

WALTERS ART MUSEUM, BALTIMORE, USA

Southern Italian red-figure pottery production
was begun in the region of Apulia during the late
5th century BCE by artists who trained in Attica
and worked both within and beyond the Greek
colony of Taras (present-day Taranto, Italy).
As it was adapted to suit local Italic market
conditions, it became increasingly distinct from
that of the Greek mainland. The volute krater
is the most characteristic Apulian shape and is
used exclusively for the tomb. This example is
the masterwork of the most important of the late
Apulian vase painters. Side A depicts Hermes
and Persephone, among others, while Side B
depicts a Campanian warrior in a naiskos (small
temple), surrounded by figures making offerings.

The Kallithea Monument

c. 320 BCE

Marble • Height: 8.3 m (27¼ ft) • Hellenistic
• From Kallithea, Attica, Greece

ARCHAEOLOGICAL MUSEUM OF PIRAEUS,
ATHENS, GREECE

This tomb, also known as the Monument of Nikeratos and Polyxenos, is one of the most extravagant of Hellenistic Athens. An inscription on the krepidoma (platform) identifies it as that of a metic (resident alien) from Istros on the Black Sea – Nikeratos – and his son, Polyxenos. The krepidoma itself is decorated with a frieze of bulls and griffin, while the high podium depicts an Amazonomachy, once brightly painted. Within the ionic naiskos (small temple) are three figures: the largest, wearing a himation, is surely Nikeratos, his son stands nude in the centre, with a slave to his left. The sculptor responsible for the tomb may have drawn inspiration from the Mausoleum at Halicarnassus (present-day Bodrum, Turkey).

Centuripe Ware Lebes Gamikos

c. 300–100 BCE
Ceramic • Height: 9.4 cm (3¾ in.)
• Hellenistic • Provenance unknown
METROPOLITAN MUSEUM OF
ART, NEW YORK CITY, USA

Highly elaborate Centuripe Ware shapes were manufactured on Sicily during the 3rd and 2nd century BCE, perhaps in response to the changes in the southern Italian red-figure vase industry. Intended specifically for the tomb, they were sometimes modelled with false lids, as here, while fine-painted decoration, often depicting women in domestic settings, was added in tempera after firing and would not have survived everyday use. Lebes gamikoi (from *gamein*, 'to marry') were vessels used specifically for marriage rituals. This example shows a bride undergoing preparations for her wedding. It may refer to the fact that its owner died unwed, or to the afterlife promised by the then-popular Cult of Dionysos.

West Slope Ware bowl

c. 300–200 BCE
Ceramic • Height: 6.2 cm (2½ in.) • Hellenistic
• Provenance unknown
MUSEUM OF FINE ARTS, BOSTON, USA

Though named for the Athenian Acropolis, West Slope Ware was produced at centres across the Greek world in a period when Attic potters and painters no longer led the industry. With naturalistic and abstract motifs in red and white overpainted on black glaze, it exemplified change in the Hellenistic adaptation and reception of pottery, and material culture more widely. The increased popularity of mould-made vessels and motifs in this period is reflected in the gorgon head that decorates this bowl. Set at the centre of a four-petalled flower and surrounded by bull heads, it may have been intended as a device to ward off evil.

Hadra vase

c. 226–225 BCE
Ceramic • Height: 42.5 cm (16¾ in.)
• Hellenistic • Provenance unknown
METROPOLITAN MUSEUM OF ART,
NEW YORK CITY, USA

Named for their prevalence within the eastern
Alexandrian cemetery of Hadra, these distinctive
hydriai (water jars) were used as urns for the ashes
of foreign dignitaries who died at the Egyptian court,
mercenary leaders and Greek soldiers who came to
Egypt with Alexander or his successor, Ptolemy I.
A small number preserve inscriptions variously
detailing the name, rank, birthplace and date of death
of their occupant. This example identifies Hieronides
of Phocaea, who died between 15 December and
13 January 226/225 BCE leading an embassy to the
court of Ptolemy III. Analysis has shown that many
of these hydriai were in fact imported to Alexandria
from workshops on Crete, reflecting the complex
and extensive character of the Hellenistic economy.

CEREMONIAL PLATE

c. 300 BCE

Gold and silver • Diameter: 25 cm (9¾ in.) • Hellenistic • From the
Temple of the Indented Niches, Ai Khanoum, Afghanistan

NATIONAL MUSEUM OF AFGHANISTAN, KABUL, AFGHANISTAN

Occupying a strategic position at the junction of the Oxus and Kokcha rivers, the Greco-Bactrian city of Ai Khanoum is an extraordinary example of the integration of Hellenistic Greek and local socio-cultural and architectural traditions, within an essentially Greek city plan. As the architecture of the palace and houses within the city replicated details seen in central Asia, Mesopotamia and Achaemenid Iran, so its principal temple followed Eastern types. The deities worshipped there, however, seem to have been Greek, or hybrid Greco-Asian forms. A fragmentary foot from the temple's cult statue suggests the worship of Zeus, perhaps in combination with the Eastern god, Mithras. There is evidence, too, of a mix of Greek and local cult practices.

Probably founded by Seleucus I in c. 300 BCE, Ai Khanoum ('Lady Moon' in Uzbek) was lost to the Nomadic Yue-tche, c. 145 BCE. Today, hundreds of pits pockmark the site – the result of illegal excavations – and the lower town has been almost completely destroyed by recent military activity.

This embossed gilt-silver plate exemplifies both the cosmopolitanism of Ai Khanoum and the hybrid nature of its art. The depiction of the goddess Cybele in a lion-drawn chariot driven by Nike (Victory) is a suitably Greek motif, as is the depiction of the sun god Helios, above. However, the barefoot priest with parasol to the rear and the second priest offering at the altar to the front are typically Eastern, and the chariot may be modelled on an Achaemenid type.

Tanagra figurine

c. 325–300 BCE
Terracotta • Height: 34 cm (13¼ in.) • Hellenistic
• From Tanagra, Boeotia, Greece
ALTES MUSEUM, BERLIN, GERMANY

Often, though not exclusively female, the
Tanagra figurine type probably developed in
Athens during the 4th century BCE as female
portraiture began to increase in popularity.
Naturalistic, sumptuously dressed and posed
in a manner both composed and self-assured,
these are not goddesses, but mortal women,
whose vibrant dress and styling conveyed their
status. Often wearing sun hats (tholia) or wreaths
and carrying fans, many may represent elite
women engaged in public ritual. Common to
cemeteries and sanctuaries, they arguably served
as a smaller, less formal version of the life-sized
female portrait statue and offer insight into the
dress and perception of Hellenistic women.

Propylon of the Sanctuary of Athena Nikephoros

c. 180 BCE

*Marble • Height: 9 m (29½ ft) • Hellenistic • From the acropolis
at Pergamon, Turkey*

PERGAMON MUSEUM, BERLIN, GERMANY

Extensive remodelling of the Sanctuary of Athena at Pergamon
under Eumenes II saw the addition of a series of new stoas
within the temenos and the construction of this propylon
(monumental gateway). Built in the style of a two-tiered stoa,
an inscription records the rededication of the sanctuary to
Athena Nikephoros, 'bringer of victory'. The frieze depicted
garlands of oak and olive, eagles and owls. As reconstructed,
the second story balustrade depicts the spoils of war including
a prow ram and ballista frame; however, it may originally
have been decorated with scenes of myth traditionally
assigned to the interior stoas.

The Alexander Sarcophagus

c. 320–300 BCE

Marble • Height: 1.9 m (6¼ ft), length at base: 3.2 m (10½ ft) • Hellenistic • From the Royal Necropolis of Sidon, Lebanon

ISTANBUL ARCHAEOLOGICAL
MUSEUM, TURKEY

The owner of this sarcophagus, a fine example of Hellenistic relief sculpture, is often identified as Abdalonymus, who later sources suggest was appointed king of Sidon by Alexander in place of his pro-Persian predecessor. Like other Sidonese sarcophagi it mirrors the form of a temple, although its sculptural subjects are overtly Greek. A battle between Greeks/Macedonians and Persians, in which Alexander himself is identified, extends halfway around the body, while hunt scenes occupy the rest. Pedimental sculpture depicts a further Greek/Persian clash and, arguably, the assassination of the Macedonian general Perdiccas (*c.* 320 BCE).

The Great Altar of Zeus

c. 170–160 BCE
Marble • Length: 36.8 m (120¾ ft), width: 34.2 m (112¼ ft)
• Hellenistic • From the acropolis at Pergamon, Turkey

PERGAMON MUSEUM, BERLIN, GERMANY

The Great Altar represents the apogee of Hellenistic baroque sculpture, a style designed to evoke a 'swaying of the soul' (psychagogia). A gigantomachy decorated the podium above eye level, interrupted only by the monumental west staircase through which dedicants accessed an internal courtyard likely housing the altar proper. An act of Pergamene propaganda perhaps inspired by a poetic source, its grandeur, intensity and vividness both referenced and surpassed its Classical predecessors. A smaller frieze at the interior colonnade offered a biography of Pergamon's founder, Telephos, and the first continuous sculptural narrative.

Glossary

Acrolith Figure of mixed materials, commonly with a torso of wood or terracotta and extremities of stone.

Acropolis The polis citadel.

Agora Public space, the commercial and administrative centre of a Greek polis.

Anthropomorphic Representing or imitating the human form.

Archon Chief magistrate.

Black Figure Pottery painting technique developed at Corinth, incorporating the addition of elements in silhouette and the incision of detail after firing.

Caryatid Female sculpture supporting an entablature.

Centaur Mythological hybrid composed of a human male torso and equine body.

Chiton Tunic-like garment formed of two parts, pinned or sewn along the edge to form openings for arms and head.

Chthonic Inhabiting, or concerning, the underworld.

Corinthian Architectural order characterized by the use of columns with tiered acanthus leaf capitals.

Cycladic Of, or concerning, the culture of the Bronze Age Cyclades.

Cyclopean Mycenaean dry-stone architectural technique utilizing very large unworked or roughly worked blocks and rubble fill.

Doric Greek dialect; architectural order characterized by the use of columns with simple capitals consisting of an echinus and abacus, and a frieze formed of triglyphs and metopes.

Egg tempera Mixture of pigment, egg yolk and water.

Filigree Ornamental metalworking technique utilizing threads and beads of gold and silver.

Fresco Technique in which pigments were applied to wet lime plaster (true or buon fresco). More durable, once dry, than those painted directly onto a dry surface (fresco secco).

Gorgon One of three female snake-haired monsters. Most commonly Medusa, killed by Perseus.

Granulation Ornamental metalworking technique characterized by the liberal addition of small gold spheres.

Helladic Of, or concerning, the culture of the Bronze Age Greek mainland.

Hexameter A line of verse consisting of six metrical feet, characteristic of epic poetry (dactylic hexameter).

Himation Large orthogonal cloak worn over the shoulder.

Hippeis Second highest Solonian property class, Athenians whose land produced 300 medimnoi of grain annually.

Ionic Greek dialect common to Asia Minor; architectural order characterized by the use of columns with volute capitals and a continuous frieze.

Lapidary Craftsperson working in both non-precious and precious stone.

Megaron Architectural unit formed of a porch, vestibule and hall.

Minoan Of, or concerning, the culture, people or language of Bronze Age Crete.

Nymphaeum Shrine dedicated to the Nymphs.

Panhellenic Of, or concerning, all of Greece.

Pankration Athletic event combining elements of wrestling and boxing.

Pentathlon Athletic event comprising discus, javelin, footrace, wrestling and jump.

Peplos Heavy garment formed of a single rectangular cloth, incorporating a characteristic overfold (apoptygma) and fastened at the shoulders with fibulae.

Phoenician Greek designation for a Levantine people of the later 2nd and 1st millennium BCE. Associated with major cities at Byblos, Tyre and Sidon.

Polis City-state, comprised of the city (asty), hinterland (chora) and the citizen body or common people (demos).

Polos Cylindrical flat-topped cap, of various sizes and sometimes associated with female deities.

Portico Colonnaded walkway, or formal entrance incorporating columns at regular intervals supporting a pediment.

Protome Modelled human- or animal-form element.

Red Figure Pottery painting technique developed at Athens, incorporating figures as reserved areas on an otherwise black glazed surface, with black glaze detail added prior to firing.

Repoussé Metalworking technique producing relief decoration by hammering from the rear side.

Retrograde Inscription written from right to left.

Satyr Male companion of Dionysos. Depicted with tail, pointed ears and often wine cups or musical instruments, commonly in a state of sexual arousal.

Sarcophagus Literally, 'flesh eater'. A coffin made from materials such as stone, terracotta or wood.

Scarification Act of scarring the body.

Shaft Grave Grave type comprising a large, deep, rectilinear pit, with stone walls to support a roof.

Sphinx Mythological hybrid composed of a human female head and winged leonine body. Guardian of Thebes in Sophocles' *Oedipus Rex*.

Stucco Fine plaster.

Tholos (Mycenaean) Monumental, stone-built semi-subterranean tomb, incorporating a main chamber with corbel-vaulted roof (thalamos), doorway (stomion) and entrance passage (dromos).

Trireme Principally a warship, characterized by three banks of oars (Greek: 'Trieres').

Tyrannicides (The) Harmodios and Aristogeiton, murderers of the brother of Athenian tyrant Hipparchos (514 BCE) and later considered heroes of democracy.

Wanax Mycenaean ruler operating as head of state (Linear B, Wa-na-ka).

Zoomorphic Representing or imitating the form of an animal or gods of animal form.

Index

*Page numbers in **bold** refer to illustrations*

Museum Index

Picture Credits

All works are courtesy of the museums listed in the individual captions. Special thanks to the Hellenic Ministry of Culture and Sports.

Acknowledgments

This book has benefited significantly from the help and advice of numerous friends and colleagues both in the UK and in Greece. Thanks are due, first and foremost, to Dr. Helen Murphy-Smith and to others whose assistance was willingly offered, and gratefully received: Dr Tristan Carter, Prof. Bill Cavanagh, Dr Katherine Harrington, Dr Gina Muskett, Dr Stephen O'Brien, Dr. Angelos Papadopoulos, Dr Chrissy Partheni, Prof. Catherine Perles, Dr. Joseph Skinner and Dr Vangelis Tourloukis.

Image acknowledgments:

Page 15.   Middle and Late Neolithic arrowheads, courtesy of Prof. Bill Cavanagh and Dr. Josette Renard.

Page 16.   Acheulean bifacial handaxe, courtesy of Dr. Vangelis Tourloukis (reproduced from Tourloukis 2010, fig. 12).

Page 17.   Mousterian leaf point, courtesy of Dr. Vangelis Tourloukis (reproduced from Tourloukis et al. 2016, Fig. 11: 7; photo by N. Thompson).

Page 18.   Bowl, courtesy of Dr Angelos Papadopoulos.

Page 20.   Beads, pendants and amulets, courtesy of Prof. Catherine Perles.

Page 200.   Prow ram, courtesy of Dr. Katherine Harrington.

First published in the United States of America in 2017 by
Thames & Hudson Inc., 500 Fifth Avenue,
New York, New York 10110

www.thamesandhudsonusa.com

© 2017 Quintessence Editions Ltd.

This book was designed and produced by
Quintessence Editions Ltd.
The Old Brewery
6 Blundell Street
London N7 9BH

Project Editor	Hannah Phillips
Designer	Michelle Kliem
Production Manager	Anna Pauletti
Editorial Director	Ruth Patrick
Publisher	Philip Cooper

Library of Congress Control Number 2016955401

ISBN 978-0-500-29349-2

Printed and bound in China